Published and distributed by

Woodbridge Press Publishing Company
Post Office Box 6189
Santa Barbara, California 93111

Copyright © 1979 by Woodbridge Press Publishing Company

Published by arrangement with ICA-förlaget AB, Stockholm
  Original title: *Gor din egen ost*
  Original Copyright © 1977 by ICA-förlaget AB

English translation and editing by Kerstin A. Shirokow,
Steven E. Hegaard/Editran, Post Office Box 2696,
Santa Barbara, California 93120

Photographs: Dan Åkerblom, Olle Åkerstrom/Ateljé Bogstedt,
Anne Nilsson and Brita Grahn

Cover: Lars Tempte

Published simultaneously in the United States and Canada

Printed in the United States of America

Library of Congress Cataloging in Publication Data

Nilsson, Anne.
    The art of home cheesemaking.

    Translation of Gor din egen ost.
    1. Cheese.   2. Cheese—Varieties.   3. Cheese—
Sweden.   I. Title.
SF271.N6513   637'.3   78-66072
ISBN 0-912800-56-9

THE ART OF Home Cheesemaking

Anne Nilsson

Published by
Woodbridge Press Publishing Company
Santa Barbara, California 93111

Contents

The Pleasure of Home Cheesemaking

Is it possible for you to make cheese at home, when you live in a city and the only milk you can get is the store-bought kind from a carton?

Yes, it is!

This book shows you just how easily you can make delicious, delicately seasoned soft cheeses, ready to eat on the spot. You will also find out how to make other exciting kinds of cheeses that gradually mellow and ripen.

Anne Nilsson gives you the recipes and the practical advice you need—and all the wonderful homemade cheeses that you make right in your kitchen will be wholesome and free from harmful additives and preservatives.

This leaf cover is both beautiful and ecological. Grape leaves, maple leaves or dandelion leaves from the garden may also be used.

Part I

Chapter 1

Pure Satisfaction in Making Your Own Cheese!

There are many ways in which milk can become cheese. It is not especially complicated or difficult to make that change happen.

The world's first cheese probably came about by mere chance. Someone may have packed food and milk in a leather bag for a long journey. After many miles of travel on horseback, when the traveler tried to drink, he discovered that his milk had curdled and formed cheese! Because of the warm weather, substances in the leather bag had turned the milk into a solid. As the bag was continuously shaken by the motion of the journey, the milk solidified still further and a thin liquid emerged. What could a hungry traveler do but eat the cheese and whey into which his milk had been transformed? A good and refreshing meal had been discovered.

The world's first cheese could also have been a sour milk cheese. If milk is left to stand in a warm place, it does not take long before it thickens and turns sour. If it is then carefully worked, the cheese substance will solidify into a lump, and the whey will separate from it. That is basically how easy it is—and the cheese will have a fresh and only slightly acid taste. Of course you will want to make your cheeses as good as possible, and you will want to make some of the many special and delicious kinds of cheeses—and in this book you will learn how.

Your first cheese may not even slightly resemble a seasoned Stilton or Camembert, but I promise you that you will not be disappointed. The very discovery that it is actually possible to make a round yellow cheese from ordinary milk will be satisfying enough to encourage you to continue experimenting.

Why Homemade Cheese?

Despite the fast pace of modern life, it is important that the art of cheesemaking be kept alive outside commercial dairies. Cheesemaking is an old craft with a long tradition. Until recently in my homeland it was an almost forgotten one. Only old women who lived on our Swedish mountain-dairy farms still knew the noble art of home cheesemaking, for their children and grandchildren had not felt the need to learn. So, in your part of the world, too, one reason for home cheesemaking is to stimulate the renaissance of interest in traditional crafts.

Another more immediate reason is that commercial dairy cheeses often contain additives whose effect on human health is still uncertain. By even partially replacing store-bought cheese with our own homemade cheese, we can diminish our consumption of these additives.

For holidays and parties too, it is nice to surprise someone with a unique gift—a beautiful Christmas cheese, a garlic cheese, or a large, ripe cheese from your kitchen. Cheesemaking, when you make the time for it, does indeed become an exciting and rewarding hobby.

Good Taste

Taste is acquired. Your homemade cheeses will have their own distinctive taste and you and your family will learn to love them—even though they may not exactly duplicate the taste of commercially made cheese. Homemade cheese will likely taste more like the natural cheese made 100 years ago in country dairies than modern store-bought cheese. There are three reasons for this: modern technology, the difference in raw materials between then and now, and the additives used by modern commercial cheese manufacturers. Homemade cheese is of course "real" cheese as much as or more so than any other we might have gotten used to, and if taste can be acquired for one, it can just as well be acquired for the other.

In the modern dairy, there are a number of different methods of measurement and sophisticated apparatus to control the manufacturing process. These would not be accessible to the person making cheese in the home, but it is just this lack of tight precision that makes homemade cheesemaking an exciting hobby with a rewarding feeling of having accomplished something "real" in an old-fashioned way.

Have Patience

Perhaps the most difficult part of making your own cheese is in allowing it to mature long enough. The actual processing is not that difficult but resisting nibbling until it has acquired its perfect flavor can be! On the other hand, the cheese must not be completely neglected, since it requires turning and it is necessary to watch for mold formation.

Aging cheese may be a long-range project; arm yourself with patience. But while waiting for the hard cheeses to ripen, you can turn your attention to the many types of fresh, soft cheeses. This book contains a variety of recipes for cheeses that may be eaten on the same day, or require only a short maturation period.

Craft and Science

A true master of cheesemaking must be thoroughly familiar with the chemical makeup of milk, as well as with bacteriology. But since milk maids managed quite well relying on their senses of taste and smell, we who make cheese for the fun of it will do well to imitate them. Therefore, the scientific aspects of cheesemaking have not been stressed here.

Cheesemaking has always been a craft; it was not until the nineteenth century that its manufacture developed into a science in large commercial dairies. However, even in the largest and most mechanized of today's dairies the "cheese master" oversees the entire process. The commercial dairies' goal of an entirely automated dairy has not yet been reached, but some of the largest ones are nearly there. Here the entire process of cheese manufacture is controlled by one person before a switchboard of panels and blinking lights that register *p*H values, weights, bacteria content, fat content, temperature and humidity levels. The "cheese master" has come a long way from running around on slippery dairy floors and turning faucets by hand. At the touch of a button the milk now somehow automatically finds its way from the tank to the next available curdling vat.

Of course, one of the greatest disadvantages in the automation of cheese manufacturing is that variations among cheeses from different localities tend to diminish or disappear altogether. Cheesemaking still does exist as a traditional craft in many countries on small farms with their own milk production; in France about 400 different varieties of cheese are still being produced and in Italy about 50. But how long will the small village dairy be able to withstand the force of the modern mechanized world?

Cheese Traditions

Sweden has interesting traditions surrounding cheesemaking, varying in different parts of the country. Mountain-dairy farms were the traditional dairies of the past, where perishable milk was changed into products that would not spoil through the winter. Cows and dairy maids would move to the mountain-dairy farm in the spring. Frequently, there were no roads, and horses would be loaded with the tools of cheesemaking. Having once reached the spring and summer pastures, the dairy maid faced a season of hard work. It was her task to care for and milk all the cows and goats and to preserve the milk in a non-perishable form. First the milk would be left to cool until the cream rose to the surface, at which time it

On the steps of "Bulla," a cottage owned jointly by the whole village, Anna Eriksson stands with a cheese, which has been drying outdoors.

Dairy maid pressing whey (mes) from cheese.

could be skimmed. By the time enough cream had been skimmed for churning into butter, that which had been saved the longest would have soured just enough to allow easy churning. When the butter had been made, buttermilk was left over; like the cream, it was slightly sour and could be used by the milk maid to make fresh cheeses.

The milk which had been skimmed was also used for cheesemaking. Rarely could dairies afford to make cheese from whole milk. The milk would be heated over a fire and homemade rennet added to allow curds to form. Over a period of time, the mixture completely separated into the cheese particles—curds and whey, a thin yellowish liquid. The curds were left to sink to the bottom of the boiling pan and then removed and pressed into a wooden mold, where the whey was squeezed from it and collected separately. Once the cheese formed from the curds had attained its proper form, it was left to dry. The whey would be boiled for several hours until it thickened to the consistency of a porridge. The final products were *mes*, or whey-butter, and cheese.

At various times during the summer, people remaining on the main farm would come up to the mountain pastures and dairy to take home the cheeses and butter made there to be sold or bartered. Milk for drinking was provided by the few cows left in the lowlands. With autumn, all the cows were brought back from the mountains to the barns of the main farm in preparation for the coming winter. Often with quick seasonal changes, there would be little time for rennet cheese to be made with the last of the season's milk. Fresh cheeses would be made instead.

Cheeses drying on the roof of a woodshed.

Some farms had a special cheese-making barn which they used when the cows returned from pasture in the fall. Other farms had cheese cellars, designed for the storing and curing of this autumn cheese.

Cheese and cheesemaking have played a large part in the traditions and culture of other peoples throughout Scandinavia. People in various regions commonly got together for cheese-making parties, and each guest would bring his own milk for a collective effort. Cheeses were often huge, with Christmas cheeses weighing up to 40 pounds each. According to one tradition, Christmas cheeses would be made during harvest time and placed underneath the sheaves of oats ready for threshing, together with aquavit and bread. Unless all the threshing was finished in time, there would be no cheese for the Christmas table!

Other Milks—Other Cheeses

Most cheeses are made from cow's milk, but other milks are often used. Goat's milk, for example, is used not only for cheese but for drinking as well. "Goat cheese" is sometimes a mixture of cow's and goat's milk. Sheep cheese is also made in some areas. Sheep cheese can be boiled with its whey and used on bread instead of butter, or made into a kind of gruel.

The Lapps milked their reindeer cows and made cheese which would keep them through the winter. Moving the pasture from the mountains to the foothills at the end of summer, the Lapps would bring back their sleds filled with reindeer cheese made during the summer. A reindeer cow will give only a tenth of a liter of milk, but it is so concentrated that the cheese yield is substantial. Reindeer milk has three times as much dry matter as cow's milk.

Part II

Chapter 2

How Milk Becomes Cheese

When the casein in milk coagulates and water is separated from it, it becomes cheese. Casein is one of several proteins contained in milk. The nutrients in milk are contained both in the cheese and the liquid whey derived from it. In cheese, the nutrients are concentrated and can be preserved for a long time. The lower the water content in cheese, the longer the nutrients will be preserved.

The principles of cheesemaking vary for different types of cheese. They all have a common basis, however: the protein of the milk must solidify and separate from the water of the milk.

In making fresh cheeses such as cream, cottage, pot or farmer, coagulation is caused by lactic acid produced by friendly bacteria in the milk.

In the making of hard cheeses it is usually rennet, an enzyme, which causes the coagulation of the casein (protein) or a modern vegetable enzyme substitute. (In this book where the word rennet is used, please understand that the publisher intends this to mean either rennet or the vegetable enzyme and recommends the latter.)

After about an hour the coagulated milk must be broken up. This is achieved by cutting the coagulated milk into cubes in the kettle, so the whey can begin to drain away. By careful manipulation, the cheese particles are prevented from lumping together before whey has sufficiently drained. This stage in the cheesemaking is called "pre-stirring." It takes place before the heating. After the milk is heated a few degrees, the next stage is the "post-stirring."

When the cheese particles have congealed enough and enough whey has drained off, the curds are removed and shaped under pressure into a cheese mold. If salt and spices are to be used, they can be worked into the curds before placing in the mold.

In order to achieve the desired bacteria culture, some dairies treat their milk with a souring agent or "culture" before the cheesemaking—because the original bacteria disappear when the milk is pasteurized. Raw milk of course needs no such souring agent. Pasteurized milk, however, usually has so few of the useful bacteria that a souring agent may be needed for the cheese to ripen properly.

There are also soft rennet cheeses, and the processing is the same as for hard cheese up to the breaking or cutting of the curds. The softness of the finished cheese is caused by the much greater water content. Thus, one has to be careful to keep as much whey as possible in the cheese. When the milk has coagulated, the cheese mixture must be either broken very little or else poured directly into the molds, without breaking. While the cheeses are left in the molds, some whey is naturally drained away.

Cheese-making from ordinary store-bought milk. Here the curds are broken or divided into four parts so the whey drains properly.

Stir carefully. This will facilitate the draining of the whey. Separate those cheese particles which seem too big.

Squeeze a spoonful of curds in your hand. If they are firm, they are ready to be taken out and molded into cheese.

Pack the curds into a mold lined with a cloth. The whey flows through the cheese and drains into a bowl.

The finished cheese, made from store-bought milk, lying in a cheese drain.

Mold (fungi) cultures may be layered into the cheese in the molds or be brushed on the outside when the cheeses are taken out of the molds. The mold helps to make the cheeses soft.

Sour cheeses are made without rennet. When a culture or other souring agent is added, such as buttermilk, yogurt, curdled milk or sour cream, the milk, given a conducive temperature, separates into curds and whey. The curds coagulated this way are softer than the ones coagulated with rennet. The milk can also sour and separate by itself without any additives, and cheese made this way can be perfectly edible. (The whey from sour cheeses should not be used for making *mes*-butter, since the sour taste remains in the whey.)

Sour cheeses are sometimes called "fresh cheeses" since they do not keep as long as the hard cheeses, but fresh cheese may also be made with rennet as a coagulation agent and thus the two terms are not necessarily interchangeable.

Whey cheeses belong to a separate group since they are made in a completely different way and contain different nutrients. When whey is boiled the water in it evaporates, and what is left in the saucepan is a more concentrated nutrient, called *mes*-butter or *mes*-cheese. This book uses *mes* as the common term associated with all whey cheeses which have a different water content from the usual cheeses.

Processed cheese is ordinary hard cheese that has been melted and mixed with additives to give it a softer or even spreadable consistency. It is often incorrectly called soft cheese but is really a processed cheese dish. The many additives make the processed cheese less desirable as food.

Chapter 3

Ingredients

Reading labels on store-bought soft cheese can encourage you to make your own cheese!

The label on a walnut cheese may read like this: "Contains hard cheese, butter walnuts, walnut essence, consistency agents, coloring and preservatives."

Ordinary hard cheese doesn't usually list its contents. If there is a label, the additives used in manufacturing are not always specified. The dairy handbook on cheesemaking says that calcium chloride may be added to regulate the curdling process. Dinitrate phosphate makes the milk rubbery if added before the calcium chloride. According to the handbook these additives are not obligatory. More common is addition of nitrates that control the growth of bacteria. Food colorings are also added. In the salt solution in which the cheeses soak to obtain a proper surface, there are also such substances as sodium hypochlorite or sodium (or calcium) sorbic acid and sodium benzoate. These substances are chemicals that slow down the mold and fermentation processes.

When we make cheese at home we ought to eliminate as many of these additives as possible. We can even do without salt, if we take care of the cheese the right way. Those who have gotten used to the taste of cheeses with additives may be a little surprised at the taste of the real, pure cheese!

Of course it is not just the additives that give cheese its distinctive taste. It is mainly the ripening process. Cheese is a living thing—bacteria and mold fungi live in it. Sometimes fermentation fungi are also present, but these are not desirable. The art of making cheese is in giving the right kind of microorganisms as good a home as possible. Undesirable guests must be discouraged, while the desirable ones must be made to feel at home, to stay and grow and fulfill their task, which is to make the cheese wholesome and good tasting.

Additives affect the life of the organisms in the cheese. So when we refrain from using them in our homemade cheese, we can not control the organisms as precisely. However, we are not completely without resources. Each step in the cheesemaking affects the life of the bacteria in the cheese and consequently the result. For example, an increase of a single degree in the temperature of the milk changes the bacteria content of the future cheese.

Milk—From the Carton or From the Cow?

A question that is always asked about cheesemaking is: is it possible to use pasteurized milk or is raw milk absolutely necessary?

Everybody who remembers the old-time recipes for cheesecake, sweet cheese and fresh cheese agrees: you have to use raw milk to get just the right taste. But it is not really as important as all that! If it is difficult to get raw cow's milk (it is licensed for sale in stores in a relatively few areas) it is quite possible to use ordinary store milk instead. However, it is necessary to "reconstitute" pasteurized milk to make it as similar to raw milk as possible. A review of some of the procedures used in processing the milk usually sold in stores will show you why.

In commercial dairies, the milk is separated into skim milk and cream, and then standardized. Standardization means that the milk gets a guaranteed fat content (for ordinary milk about 3 or 4 grams of fat to 100 grams of milk). Either the skim milk is mixed with cream until the correct fat content is reached, or else it is mixed with whole (unseparated) milk.

Then the milk must be pasteurized by heating. On pasteurization, the bacteria, viruses and enzymes which cannot stand the high temperature are killed. Unfortunately, useful substances are also killed—for instance, the lactic acid bacteria which are necessary for cheesemaking. These bacteria must be put back into the milk in order to make cheese from pasteurized milk. Fortunately, every refrigerator can contain these bacteria—in the form of buttermilk!

Even milk which dairies have set aside for cheesemaking is pasteurized, the desirable bacteria being added later. This is done to kill decomposing and other undesirable bacteria. It is important to the dairies to produce uniform cheese from one day to the next.

In many countries not all milk for cheesemaking is pasteurized. The Swiss Emmenthal cheese and the French Gruyere are made from unpasteurized milk. In such cases, cleanliness is of the utmost importance to the outcome of the cheesemaking—in the barn, during transportation of the milk, and in the dairy.

Another procedure in processing milk in commercial dairies is homogenization. This process diffuses the fat particles so that cream cannot form and rise to the top of the milk in the cartons. Thus, if regular store-bought milk is used in making cheese at home, whether it is to be hard or soft rennet cheese or fresh cheese, it is quite unnecessary to add extra cream. The fat is already there. The fat, of course, is not necessary at all—it simply makes the cheese a little richer. Cheese has been made for centuries from skim milk. It is necessary to add cream only in order to make an especially rich, luxurious cream cheese.

Genuine Cow's Milk From the Farm

For those who live in the country it is not difficult to obtain genuine, untreated cow's milk. If the dairy is truly sanitary, it is possible to make the very finest cheeses without pasteurizing the milk, for all the natural substances are in the milk. If there is a choice between pasteurized milk or sanitary raw milk, the latter is far more desirable for making cheese. Such milk may be available in health food stores or other stores as "certified raw milk."

With luck, you may find a country source of clean, untreated milk. Of course, harmful bacteria may still exist in the milk, and milk which isn't cooled deteriorates quickly. Thus, milk should not be left standing—cheesemaking should start immediately after the milk is brought home. Some home cheesemakers first of all add a souring agent (buttermilk, yogurt, etc.) even when the milk is not pasteurized. This is done in order to

Peggy from Björnsarv, Sweden gives about 5 gallons of milk a day.

make the lactic acid bacteria reproduce more quickly, and also serves to eliminate the unnecessary or harmful ones.

Milk still warm from the cow facilitates cheesemaking since it doesn't need to be heated to the temperature necessary for adding the rennet. If such fresh milk is not available, the milk you have, perhaps from an evening milking, can be used. It should be kept cool overnight, skimmed the next morning and mixed with the milk from the morning milking. The "older" milk tends to speed up the ripening process (the way the souring agent does). It was common practice among old-time home cheesemakers to mix the evening milk with morning milk, and this is practiced even today by some dairies. For similar reasons summer milk is easier to make cheese from than winter milk.

There are instances when cheese made from raw milk ferments during the first days of ripening. This is caused by an excess of harmful fermentation-causing bacteria. The cheese tastes bitter, smells bad and is not edible. To avoid this, two things should be remembered:

1. Cleanliness—from farm to kitchen!

2. If there is any uncertainty about that, the milk must be pasteurized (heated to 161°F. for 15 seconds, or 143°F. for 30 seconds) and then quickly cooled. This kills the fermentation-causing bacteria, as is done in the dairies.

Warning Against Antibiotics

Cows that have been treated with antibiotics against inflammation of the udder or any other illness retain traces of the medicine in their milk for a few days after treatment. Apart from the fact that milk with antibiotics is undesirable as food, the ability of the milk to curdle is impaired by the addition of even the smallest amount of antibiotics. After a cow has been treated, one should wait at least three or four days before using its milk for cheesemaking. However, it can be used for other things.

Rennet and Vegetable Enzymes

Hard cheeses and most soft cheeses require the use of an enzyme, usually rennet. There has been real progress in production of various substitutes, rennetless processes, which will be discussed later.

A creamy delicious blue cheese is ready to enjoy. The white cheese is a fresh goat cheese. Behind it lies a ripened goat cheese, surrounded by two yellow cheeses from cow's milk, and a goat mes-cheese, made from whey.

Commercial rennet can be bought as liquid, paste or tablet in stores where chemicals are sold, some health food stores, drugstores, and from the sources listed in the back of this book. You may also be able to use junket tablets (*not* junket mix) with a little experimentation. To test the quality of the rennet, pour a few drops into a cup of lukewarm milk. If the rennet is of good quality, it won't be long before the milk curdles.

Many plant enzymes and other products have been tried over the centuries but only recently have micro-

High quality cultures, rennets and vegetable rennets are available from druggists, health food stores or suppliers in the Appendix.

On the drain board in front there is a small cheese from a dairy made from rennet and milk. Since the surface hasn't dried yet the cheese is still white. A jar of cow mes-butter, a ripened goat cheese, a brown goat mes-cheese, and a cheese from cows' milk with a yellowed surface are surrounded by cheese molds from different periods: handmade wooden troughs, a modern mold of fiber-glass and plastic, and an ordinary can with the bottom removed.

The Easter cheese is resting on a bed of yellow straw, as it is being baked in the oven. Made from the recipe for Easter cheese.

bial-fungal, vegetable-based materials been developed that work as well as rennet.

These new fungal "proteinases" have proven to be very successful—particular that from *Mucor miehei*. This substance is the basis of most of the new vegetable rennet tablets.

One of these is "Hannilase" brand vegetable rennet tablets. They may be ordered (send a check with order) in vials of 12 tablets at $2.95 (1978 price) from: Chr. Hansen's Laboratory, 9015 W. Maple St., Milwaukee, WI 53214. This company also has addresses in England, Canada, Australia (see the Appendix).

A vegetable enzyme similar to (and older than) that based on *Mucor miehei* is "Emporase," based on *Mucor pusillus*. It is sold by Dairyland Food Laboratories, 620 Progress Ave., Waukesha, WI 53187. Dairyland has pioneered also in the development of products known as lipase enzymes for the making of various Italian cheeses.

Actually a substantial proportion of commercial cheeses are being made today with this vegetable-based enzyme and it is the publisher's belief that the reader of this book will wish to utilize it in preference to animal-based rennet wherever possible.

One of the most successful cheesemaking companies using such materials in the United States is Health Valley of Montebello California. They manufacture and sell through health food stores and other outlets a wide variety of cheeses including mild, medium and sharp cheddar; several varieties of jack cheese, longhorn, munster, and Swiss—proof enough that the vegetable enzymes can produce truly fine cheeses.

Cultures to "Ripen" the Milk

If you are using milk that is pasteurized, it is necessary to replace the destroyed bacteria with new ones. You can use a commercial culture or you may use ordinary buttermilk (store-bought or homemade), yogurt or other sour milk products. The lactic acid bacteria in these cultures or products help to coagulate the milk, and to preserve the cheese and give it the proper taste. They eliminate, among other things, different kinds of bacteria that cause fermentation.

The culture is added to the milk before the rennet. The period between the adding of the culture and the adding of the rennet is called the ripening period of the milk. To ripen the milk means to achieve a proper balance among the various bacteria added to the milk.

If buttermilk directly from the refrigerator is mixed into the milk, it will take a little while before the bacteria start to reproduce, for lactic acid bacteria have an incubation period. During that time other harmful bacteria may also grow. For this reason the lactic acid bacteria should be activated as soon as possible.

This can be expedited by using a pure culture. You can buy this (see product list in back of this book) or you can make a culture. For a cheese to be made of 2½ gallons of milk, enough culture can be made by boiling 3 ounces of milk (to sterilize it) and quickly cooling it to 62-65°F. Mix into it 1 tablespoon of buttermilk and keep in a warm place until the next day. It may, for instance, be kept in a prewarmed Thermos bottle. This is your "culture."

The next day mix the lactic acid culture with the milk from which the cheese is to be made, heated to 82°F. After 15-20 minutes of ripening, add the rennet or other enzyme.

It is possible to make an even "purer" culture from sour milk for continuing use. First keep a cup of milk in a warm place until it sours. After about two days when the milk is sour, it must be "transplanted." Boil about a cup of milk, cool to room temperature, and mix it with the sour milk. When this milk has soured, the "transplanting" is repeated until a thoroughly sour milk is obtained that smells freshly acid. Sour milk obtained this way has a very high content of lactic acid bacteria and the lowest possible content of harmful bacteria. As soon as a new culture has soured, it should be cooled and kept in the refrigerator. For continuing use, it should be transplanted every other day so as to remain fresh.

Mold Cultures

Blue cheese and Camembert—it is quite possible to make these gourmet cheeses at home! Maybe they won't turn out exactly like the imported ones but the result is good enough to be well worth the trouble. Homemade blue cheese is, by the way, as "real" as the store-bought variety. The only "real" Roquefort cheese, on the other hand, is the cheese that comes from the caves of Roquefort, France.

Mold cultures are sold in almost any dairy case— any piece of blue cheese is actually a mold culture! The same goes for all the other kinds of mold-cultured cheeses sold commercially. How to make them is described later in the sections on cultured cheeses.

You can also buy a pure mold culture from the sources listed in the back of this book.

Salt and Flavoring

Salt acts as a preservative as well as flavoring in the making of cheese. By using just the right amount of salt, dairies can accurately control the growth of the various bacteria. Homemade cheeses are usually salted less accurately. Salt is either put on the outside to protect the cheese against outside bacteria, or it can be mixed into the cheese before it is put into the mold.

Most cheeses age quite well without any salt. Thus if you must or prefer to restrict salt intake, it is possible to leave out the salt completely, in which case lactic acid bacteria are relied on to destroy the harmful bacteria.

Some common spices used in home cheesemaking are cumin and cloves. Ginger is also used. In order to get more taste from the cumin seeds, they can be softened by pouring boiling water over them—before mixing them with the cheese. This is better than grinding them, since ground cumin seeds would make the cheese appear to have "dirt" particles. Crush cloves into small pieces, then pour boiling water over them as with the cumin seeds. In dairies all the spices are boiled so as to prevent mold and fermentation cultures. Aquavit is sometimes used to rub away mold on the outside of the cheese. Herbs, nuts, pepper and garlic are often added to soften cheeses. The seasoning of fresh cheeses is described in a later section.

You don't need to buy a lot of utensils to make cheese. A colander and a tin can with its bottom removed are all you need. A plate as a lid, a stone to weigh it down and a tray with high edges to keep the whey which drains from the cheese from spilling. Simple and inexpensive!

Chapter 4

Tools for Cheesemaking

It is not necessary to buy complicated machinery or expensive tools in order to make cheese. The supplies needed, with the possible exception of a large kettle, can usually be found in an ordinary kitchen. Not even a cheese mold is really necessary for the very first attempts. Any "mold" at all can be used to shape the cheese.

Simple Tools for Your First Attempts at Cheesemaking

Here are some tools you will need: a large kettle with lid, a long-handled stirring tool, a thermometer, measuring spoons, a knife, a strainer, a bowl for molding and cheesecloth.

A large kettle is necessary because you need a lot of milk to make a practical amount of cheese. One quart of cow's milk yields about 4 or 5 ounces of cheese. It is important that a hard cheese which has to mature not be too small and thin, otherwise only dry surfaces remain when the cheese has matured enough. Two gallons of milk will yield a cheese weighing about 2 pounds, and that is a good size to start with. Of course, the size of the cheese to be made depends upon how much milk is available and the kettle can vary in size proportionately. Generally, 1 pound of hard cheese requires about 10 pounds of milk—a little less than 5 quarts.

For goat cheese the proportions are about the same. For sheep cheese, however, a 3-quart kettle is enough. The yield is much greater, because sheep's milk has a much greater proportion of solids.

A tool to stir is necessary so that the milk is heated uniformly. A long wooden fork or perforated spoon should be used. An ordinary wooden spoon may also be used, but sometimes causes the milk to splash if stirred too rapidly.

A thermometer is needed to measure the temperature of the milk before the rennet or other enzyme is added. An ordinary room thermometer may be used if a food thermometer is not available, although a cheese thermometer is best. Like all the other tools, it must be scrupulously clean.

A tablespoon and a teaspoon will be needed to measure the rennet. The kettle must be covered with a lid while the milk is curdling (a towel may be used in place of a lid) to prevent the milk from losing too much heat.

A knife or spatula with a blade as long as the depth of the kettle is needed for cutting up the curds.

Eventually the curds are taken out of the kettle with a spoon or with clean hands and are set out to drain. A colander or a large strainer is perfect.

In fact, for a mold you can simply use the strainer or

colander itself. Another kind of mold is a nicely designed open, straw work basket. It will give the cheese an attractive pattern. It is also possible to simply bore holes in a plastic jar or a can. Before long you'll be looking at every kind of can or container trying to figure out how it can be used as a cheese mold!

Cheese molds are usually made of wood. Molds like some mentioned above that are not made of wood can allow heat to escape too quickly, cooling the cheese, which in turn prevents adequate drainage of the whey. In such a case you must cover the mold with a cloth (or else let the whey remain in the bowl under the colander or strainer to retain some of its heat). A cheesecloth in the mold is ideal, or an ordinary linen towel or any other piece of cloth the size of the mold may be used.

This simple homemade cheese mold is both glued and screwed together. It is on its side to show how the bottom is made. The measurements are in the text, but the mold can be made to any size.

The cloth isolates the cheese substances and facilitates draining of the whey—because of its porosity as well as by means of the impressions it makes on the surface of the cheese—something like drainage channels.

If you plan to save the whey, the mold should be left in a towel on a tray with high edges since whey will be constantly seeping from the cheese. The bowl or tray has to be emptied often. If you don't plan to use the whey, the mold can also be put on a cutting board in the sink. Then the whey will go directly down the drain. If the cheese must be molded under pressure (the recipes will tell you this), a plate can be put upside down on the colander and a weight put on top.

Pyramid Molds for Soft Cheeses

Soft rennet cheeses need a long time to drain. If the cheese and the cheesecloth constantly touch the accumulated whey, proper drainage can't take place, since the cheese will reabsorb the whey. In the old days the cheese mold was put in a hollow wooden drain. The whey flowed down into a bucket, and the cheese remained dry all the time. We, too, must be sure to keep the cheese dry. On the tray or in the bowl which collects the whey, place an object to prevent the cheese above from touching the accumulating whey. This can be a wooden board or a plate with a completely flat bottom, turned upside down.

Dessert cheeses may be made in small smooth molds without any cheesecloth for drainage. In that case some other piece of coarsely woven cloth should be placed between the mold and the drainage board in the bowl. The cloth will serve as a drainage net, and should not touch the whey in the bottom of the bowl. The cloth will make a pattern on the cheese. On certain exclusive foreign cheeses such a pattern can be seen, made from the straw mats on which the cheeses rest during the drainage of the whey.

Thin metal and plastic molds are often so light that they are easily knocked over, which of course means that the cheese will have to be put back and molded all over again. To prevent this put a weight on top that presses the mold against the table—a plate with a heavy object on top will do nicely. The curds must not be loaded so high that their own weight presses them down; soft cheeses should be molded without pressure.

Tools for Making Fresh (Acid) Cheeses

Since fresh cheeses don't have to drain as carefully as the cheeses which must ripen, not as many utensils are necessary. All that is needed is a saucepan large enough to hold the amount of cheese planned, a wooden fork or something else to stir with, and draining utensils. Here the requirements vary somewhat, but you can find everything necessary in most kitchens. A strainer or colander with a bowl underneath to catch the whey is adequate. A piece of cloth such as a towel or a handkerchief may be put in the strainer. You can also tie the cloth over a pitcher or let it hang as a bundle over the kitchen sink. When doing this put a container underneath if you wish to save the whey.

To give soft cheeses a pretty shape, try using a little bowl with a thin cloth in it to press the curds after they are drained.

Tools for the Serious Home Cheesemaker

For those who wish to make cheese on a more or less regular basis, it would be worthwhile to invest in utensils used specifically for making cheese.

A 2-3 gallon kettle or one even larger should be acquired. (Goat owners who make cheese for sale usually have 8-15 gallon kettles.) To make cheese from cow's milk that weighs over 20 pounds, kettles which hold *more* than 2-3 gallons are necessary.

A long thermometer is indispensable for those who wish to make cheesemaking an art. One degree's difference in the heating of the milk can greatly change the cheese. Thus the scale on the thermometer must be clearly visible, and it must be long enough to reach to the bottom of the milk (even so, it is necessary to stir the milk properly to achieve uniform heat).

To measure the amount of rennet, a measuring cup or spoons indicating milliliters or fractions of ounces should be used.

A perforated ladle from which the whey can easily drain is useful to remove the curds from the kettle. In making soft rennet cheeses the curds must be placed very carefully in fairly narrow molds. For this purpose a ladle with a 90-degree angle between the handle and the ladle is extremely helpful. Such a ladle can easily be lowered to the bottom of the narrow mold.

There are many kinds of cheese molds. Metal cans with their bottoms removed are perfect; an alternative is to perforate the bottoms and sides of the cans, using a hammer and nail (from the inside). Small cans are good for soft rennet cheeses, and bigger cans, coffee cans for instance, should be used for 2-pound hard cheeses or for the flatter cheesecakes made with mold cultures.

In the past cheese molds were always made of wood. Wood isolates heat and helps the cheese keep warm longer, whereas plastic and metal molds cool the cheese and thus retard drainage of the whey. Thus it is important to cover a nonwood mold with a thick cloth in order to prevent heat from escaping.

It is not at all difficult to make square wooden molds. Each one should be made like a drawer without bottom, with its sides glued and screwed together. Since the wood expands when the mold becomes damp from the whey, it must be sturdy. A mold simply put together with nails will soon be useless. Bacteria can find their way through the nail holes and cause the wood to deteriorate. The best way of all is to use wooden plugs to put the sides together, as well as water-proof glue.

The size of the mold depends on the size of the cheese to be made, or on the size of the kettle available for heating the milk. A mold with inside measurements about 6 inches square by 5 inches deep can be used to make cheeses weighing 4-6 pounds. For that size cheese an 8-gallon kettle is needed for the milk. Such a mold can also be used for flatter cheeses such as blue cheeses and Port Salut. The boards for the mold should be about 5 inches wide and about half an inch thick. The photograph on page 41 shows how the mold is made. In the old days the sides of the molds were dovetailed together, as shown on page 41.

The advantage of molds that can be taken apart is, above all, that they are more hygienic. No leftover whey or curds can remain on the corners and they are easier to wash carefully and to dry quickly.

You should form hard cheeses as compactly as possible, which is a fact that must be considered in

Soft dessert cheeses with your own individual flavor are easy and inexpensive to make. Here the cheese is layered with spices in cans without bottoms.

A stone or other weight presses the mold against a support to prevent the curds from pouring out and upsetting the mold.

A chive-cheese and a green pepper-cheese are ready after two days in their molds. They can be eaten right away, but will taste better if left to ripen for a while in the refrigerator, wrapped in foil or plastic wrap.

deciding their measurements. A short and thick hard cheese is preferable to a long thin one, in order to diminish the surface susceptible to mold. Soft cheeses may be made flatter—like Brie, which is often made in the shape of a cake.

The bottomless wooden mold must not fit too snugly on the table on which it is resting—the whey must escape. This may be achieved by making the support strips in the corners slightly longer than the sides. You can get the same result by rounding off the bottom edges of the mold.

Cheeses weighing 2 pounds or less can easily be molded and drained in a large strainer or colander. Frequently turning the cheese around during the first hours gives it a nice round shape. Old-fashioned colanders which have feet can hold larger cheeses.

Some cheeses are made without a hard mold at all. The curd is simply put into a towel which is twisted so that the cheese particles are pressed together. The cheese is then placed in a bucket (because of the dripping whey) with a weight on top for a day or two. It should be turned from time to time. Then the cheese is wrapped in a cloth.

When wooden molds are used, a plate with a weight on top may be used as a lid in order to press the cheese more evenly.

Cheesecloth is put inside cheese molds. You may also use muslin (with all the starch and filler washed out) if you wish a stronger cloth. One purpose of the cloth is to slightly perforate the surface of the cheese in order to help the whey escape properly. The cloth also makes a design on the surface of the cheese, so it is important to wrap it smoothly and with as few folds as possible. For square cheeses a cloth especially made to fit the mold is preferable. Another way is to use two narrower strips of cloth and put them crosswise in the mold, resulting in a double layer of cloth in the bottom and a single layer on the sides. If a strainer or colander is used, the cloth can be stretched in order to avoid creases. For this purpose a loosely woven cloth is preferable. The coarser the cloth, the bolder the design on the surface of the cheese. Cheese dries more quickly if its surface has a design than if it is smooth.

To drain the whey, real old-fashioned cheese drains are of course the best. They used to be made from thick wooden slabs, with a hollow "basin." Since the basin edges were carved smooth, there were no places for the whey to stick and get dry and for bacteria to thrive, as would be the case if the edges were simply attached to the wooden slabs.

If it is too difficult to make a proper wooden cheese drain (or find an old-fashioned one) an ordinary drip pan will do. If the pan is to be used exclusively for cheese, it can be adapted somewhat. Make an opening in one side, so whey can leave the pan as it leaves the cheese. Someone handy with a power drill or a hacksaw and file can probably take care of that.

Weights should be kept handy in case the cheese is to be pressed. Ordinary stones of selected sizes and shapes will do.

If cheeses are to be made on a regular basis a storage space for the ripening of the cheeses will be necessary. Kitchen counters, bookcases and ordinary tables may be used, but if the whole house starts smelling of cheese, other means have to be provided. For cheeses which need ordinary room temperature a special kitchen cupboard may be set aside. Cheeses which need lower temperatures may be stored in basement cupboards. Fortunately, most cheeses will ripen well at room temperature, which is also the quickest way. Once a cheese has acquired its proper smell and taste, it should be put in a cooler place, together with cheeses which need a longer time to ripen. For further details see the section, "Ripening of Hard Cheese."

Write It Down!

Always keep a notebook handy and write down everything you do in your first cheese-making attempts. Otherwise it will be very difficult to remember a month later exactly how you did it.

First write down the date on which the cheese was made, then how much milk was used, if it was skim or whole milk, and, if curdled milk was used, the ripening time and amount. Write down the exact temperature of the milk when the rennet is added, the time required for curdling and "post-stirring" and the temperature of the whey during the post-stirring. Write down *how* the curds were taken out of the kettle, if the cheese was salted and how long it stayed in the mold. Be sure to make a note of even the smallest details of your cheesemaking.

If your cheese turned out perfect, you must try to make the next cheese exactly the same way. If it didn't, one or perhaps several steps in the cheese-making process must be changed—maybe longer post-stirring, or a higher temperature. Even the facts that pertain to the ripening should be noted: times and temperatures, and if and when mold and cracks appear. When different kinds of cheeses are made, it is especially important to have notes—to be able to tell them apart! That way you learn as much as possible from both successful and unsuccessful attempts at making cheese.

Part III

Chapter 5

Start By Making A Fresh Cheese

Before attempting to make a proper hard cheese it is good practice to make a fresh cheese. Fresh cheeses can be made more quickly and it is possible to experiment with them on a smaller scale. The basics of cheesemaking are easily seen in the making of fresh cheese: the casein, which is part of the protein in the cheese, forms curds that are the cheese particles and the whey separates from them. A fresh cheese can be eaten as soon as the whey has properly separated from the cheese, and the eager novice cheesemaker can almost immediately enjoy the results of his first attempt.

What Is a Fresh Cheese?

Fresh cheeses are generally those which should not be ripened for any length of time. There are fresh cheeses that may be ripened and stored, but those aren't the kind we usually think of when we are describing fresh cheeses. They are sometimes called acid, or sour, cheeses, because a souring agent has been used instead of the rennet usually used in cheeses to be ripened and stored.

When milk is kept warm, it sours. This is caused by lactic bacteria that produce lactic acid, which makes the milk thicken. Lactic bacteria are not harmful for human consumption; on the contrary, these are the very same bacteria used for certain preservation purposes, as in sauerkraut. Decaying bacteria, on the other hand, are not desirable, and if milk is left a really long time it may spoil. Usually, however, lactic bacteria replace the decaying bacteria, making sour milk not harmful but rather healthful for human consumption. It is possible to cultivate lactic bacteria. Such cultures are used by dairies to regulate the acid content and flavor in cheese. Curdled milk is one kind of cultivated acid. Here the decaying and other harmful bacteria have been replaced by the lactic bacteria.

Many souring agents may cause the milk to congeal: the acid already in curdled milk and buttermilk, yogurt and naturally aged milk, citric acid, vinegar, etc. Some dairy cheeses are made with a lot of acid and little rennet. Thus they are called acid-rennet cheeses.

In areas where the tradition of making fresh cheese is still alive, the term "fresh cheese" is used without further qualification as to how it is made. The cheese may be soured with curdled milk or naturally, of its own accord. My choice of names for the various fresh cheeses has been made for purely practical reasons—I am in no way suggesting that different local names are wrong. The names of various fresh cheeses have been passed on from generation to generation and although the cheeses may be the same, the names can be different depending on where they came from.

Natural Fresh Cheese Without Souring Agents

I got this recipe for fresh cheese from a Finnish woman named Lisa Wetonen, who has lived in Sweden for many years. It is made with no additives except cream. Lisa learned to make this cheese from her mother and her grandmother used the same recipe. Natural fresh cheese has been made all over Scandinavia and probably all over the world using a simple recipe something like this one.

Lisa never uses less than about 5 quarts of milk and she prefers "real cow's milk from the barn." When such milk is not readily available, she uses ordinary store-bought milk mixed with a half-pint of whipping cream. This way the taste and the consistency of the fresh cheese turn out the best.

For the first attempt it is preferable to make a smaller cheese, using perhaps 2 quarts of milk and half a cup of whipping cream.

Keep the mixture of milk and cream in a saucepan, covered with a lid, in a fairly warm place; for example, on top of the oven when it is being used, or at the side of the stove.

Lisa's mother kept her saucepan on the wood-burning stove. Old-fashioned wood stoves with rings didn't get as hot as the modern ones. It is important

Curdled-milk cheese is made from ordinary curdled milk which has been heated just a little and poured into a strainer with a straining cloth inside.

that the milk not get too hot; if the heat only comes from underneath, it will be necessary to stir from time to time so that the milk becomes uniformly warm. The stirring must stop, however, when the milk starts to smell sour, so as not to destroy the curds. Some stoves have an area for plate warming which may be used to keep the milk at the right temperature, and the top of some refrigerators is warm enough.

Keeping the milk in a warm place causes it to sour more rapidly. It must not become so sour that it turns bluish and moldy, which may happen if it is left to sour too slowly. After at least two days the milk will usually have thickened and will be sour. It is then time to "break up" the large congealed mass into pieces. With a spatula the curd in the saucepan is gently broken up into pieces of about 2 inches in diameter.

Put the saucepan on low heat. The curds should not get hotter than 102°F. You should be able to touch them with your fingers.

When the whey has separated from the curds, take the saucepan off the stove to cool to room temperature. When the curds are cool, put a cloth in a colander and pour the curds into it, so that the whey can separate. Carefully twist the cloth to squeeze out the last of the whey. Replace it in the colander, put a weight on top and set in a cool place overnight. Next morning the cheese is ready to eat! If any is left over it may be frozen.

Curdled-Milk Cheese

Fresh cheese made with milk alone I have chosen to call simply "curdled-milk cheese." It is easy to make and the result closely resembles a German and East European type of cheese similar to cottage cheese, but smoother and with a sour taste.

When curdled milk is strained at room temperature the curds remain in the strainer while the whey drips into the pot below. The following day the cheese is ready to be eaten, and the whey may be used in baking bread.

I make this fresh cheese from milk to which some already curdled milk has been added as a souring agent. It tastes quite different from fresh cheese made just from naturally soured milk. The reason is that the bacteria cultures are somewhat different. Curdled-milk cheese is made in about the same way as natural fresh cheese except that, instead of a half cup of whipping cream, add about that much milk that has already curdled naturally. The resulting new curd is strained so that the whey separates. The fresh cheese is left in the strainer until well drained, after which it can be seasoned if desired.

To facilitate the separation of the cheese particles from the whey, the curdled milk should be slowly heated on low heat. The milk should be stirred while heating in order to become uniformly warm. The milk must not become too hot—again, not over 102°F. When the curdled milk turns granular it is ready to strain. You can usually tell if it is granular simply by observing the edges of the saucepan.

The next step is straining the curdled milk to separate the whey from the curds. Here are several ways to do it.

1. Place a cloth into a colander or a big strainer. Set the colander on top of a bowl where the whey will be able to drip.

2. Tie a cloth over a pitcher so that a hollow is formed in the opening of the pitcher. The curds will stay in the cloth and the whey will drip into the pitcher.

3. Pour the curdled milk into a cloth in a colander, and tie the edges of cloth together with a string. Then hang the bundle on a hook over the sink, and let the whey drip into a bowl underneath. The bowl with the colander or pitcher should be kept cool while the whey is dripping.

After a couple of hours of draining the cheese is ready; it is not necessary to press or to ripen it. You may however season it. (See the section, "Flavoring Fresh Cheeses".) It may be cut into slices to put on bread or into pieces to eat with fruits and vegetables. Mixed thoroughly with some ordinary curdled milk, it will become spreadable.

Curdled-Milk Cheese the Estonian Way

Those cheese lovers like me who hate milk kettles that boil over and saucepans with burned milk in the bottom can rejoice over this recipe from Estonia.

In a saucepan, boil 3 quarts of water; remove from heat. Pour in 1 or 2 quarts of naturally curdled milk. When the curdled milk touches the hot water, the cheese particles separate from the whey. Strain as previously described.

The disadvantage of this method is that the whey is wasted since it is diluted with so much water.

Mild Fresh Cheese with Curdled Milk

This fresh cheese begins to seem more like the hard cheeses. It is almost chewy and it can readily be sliced. Sour milk makes harder curds if it is heated to a very high temperature.

To try this cheese, heat 1 quart of sweet milk to just below the boiling point (about 205°F.). Remove the saucepan and mix in 1¼ cups of curdled milk. Let the mixture stand a few minutes and then pour it into a sieve lined with coarsely woven cloth. (The curds will be larger with this method.) The cloth makes it easier to remove the whole cheese from the sieve as well as giving the cheese a nice pattern. It can be carefully

Fresh cheese made from curdled milk or buttermilk may be strained through an ordinary sieve without a cloth.

removed after both cheese and cloth have been placed on a plate. At this point the cheese should be fairly solid and the dripping should have stopped.

If more than just a taste test is desired, the proportions should be increased. Two cups of curdled milk will curdle 6 cups of sweet milk, and the result is a cheese small enough to fit a saucer. The original recipe calls for one quart of curdled milk and three quarts of sweet milk, which yields a cheese more worthy of the effort.

Fresh Cheese Made With Buttermilk

In the old days any type of cheese could be called buttermilk cheese as long as it used buttermilk as an ingredient. In this book "buttermilk cheese" refers to cheese made exclusively from buttermilk. Fresh cheese with sweet milk *and* buttermilk I call "fresh cheese with buttermilk."

When the time came to move from the mountain-dairy back to the farm, nobody had time to make proper cheese after the last milking. Instead the dairy maids made fresh cheese that was curdled with buttermilk left over when the cream had been churned into butter. Since cream from several milkings had been collected in order to get enough to churn, the cream had time to sour a little. This was important when fresh cheese was to be made from it. Buttermilk that comes from completely fresh cream doesn't curdle. On the contrary, the buttermilk should be so sour that it thickens. Fortunately, in the United States buttermilk is sold in most grocery stores. However, store-bought buttermilk may have to be left at room temperature for a while until it is really thick and sour.

Once the buttermilk is thick, sweet milk must be added to it. The procedure is about the same as for fresh cheese with curdled milk. The approximate proportions are one to six, depending on the acid content of the buttermilk. If there is only 1 quart of buttermilk available, it might be safer to use it in proportions of one to five. Otherwise one might end up with 7 quarts of a milk mixture that won't curdle. (If that happens, the mixture should be left at room temperature until it thickens, then carefully heated and strained in the same way as for making curdled-milk cheese.)

A little test cheese can be made from 2½ cups of sweet milk and ½-¾ cup of buttermilk. The yield will be a cheese weighing about 5½ ounces, like a small dessert cheese. For 3 quarts of sweet milk, between ½ and 1 quart of buttermilk should be used, and for 6 quarts of sweet milk, 2 to 3 quarts of buttermilk.

To make the cheese: Boil the sweet milk. Stand by the stove the whole time and stir with a wooden fork, touching the bottom of the saucepan, so the milk won't stick. Just as the milk is coming to a boil, add the buttermilk and remove the saucepan from the stove. Stir the mixture a few more times in order to mix the buttermilk well with the milk. Then leave it all standing for a while and watch the formation of the cheese particles—for they are much bigger than when curdled milk is heated. If the whey still has the color of milk, it means that more curds could be formed. Heat it again without stirring and add more buttermilk.

When you think you have the right proportions, strain the mixture through a large sieve. The cheese particles will be so big that no cheesecloth is necessary. When the whey has stopped dripping through the

The morning milking has been finished and the cows are put out to graze. (Harsen's mountain dairy in northern Sweden.)

sieve, the cheese should be turned in order to facilitate drainage from the top.

When all the whey has drained from the cheese and it has become solid, it should be put on a platter and kept cool. It may be served whole or cut into slices.

In the old days special cheese baskets were used for this kind of cheese. The baskets were woven from birch or spruce roots and a pattern with openings was placed on the bottom of the basket, giving the finished cheese a pretty design.

If you follow the recipe above, heating the milk to the boiling point and then curdling with buttermilk, the fresh cheese will be white. A rust-yellow color can be obtained by boiling the sweet milk longer before adding the buttermilk. This color is caused by the reaction of the lactose with the protein when heated, and appears in all mes products. Sometimes a cinnamon stick is included. Fresh yellow cheese is sweeter in taste since the milk has boiled longer.

Buttermilk Cheese

Just as it is possible to make fresh cheese from curdled milk alone, it is also possible to make it solely from buttermilk.

Let your buttermilk sour in a saucepan until it has the consistency of curdled milk, then carefully heat it until it has reached a lukewarm temperature. It must not feel hot to the touch when one sticks a finger in it. Remember to watch the sides of the saucepan so you can see when the whey is separating from the cheese particles. When that happens the buttermilk should be strained.

Buttermilk cheese is drained just like curdled-milk cheese. When the whey has stopped dripping the fresh cheese is ready. Buttermilk cheese is softer, easier to spread and has a stronger taste than fresh cheese made from sweet milk and buttermilk.

Fresh Yogurt Cheese

Fresh cheese that is soured with yogurt tastes refreshing but not strong. Combining 3 cups of sweet milk and ¾ cup of unflavored yogurt yields just the right size test cheese. It is made like any other fresh cheese: boil the milk, then mix in the yogurt, remove from heat and let stand for a while. If the whey is still white, the mixture can be boiled some more. When the whey starts to simmer, the rest of the cheese particles separate. Pour it all into a sieve. The cheese is ready almost immediately.

Yogurt Cheese

Heat yogurt, stirring slowly all the time until it is warm to the touch. Then pour into a cloth which has been placed into a sieve. Lift up the corners of the cloth and tie them with a string. Hang the bag on a hook and put a bowl underneath to catch the whey. Next morning put the cheese into a bowl or mold it into a round cheese. Since it is made from concentrated yogurt, it has a strongly sour taste. Finely chopped mild herbs may be added to the curds, or the finished cheese may be rolled in sesame or poppy seeds.

Fresh Cheese With Lemon

Anyone who has put both milk and lemon in tea knows that the milk then curdles. What is floating on top of the tea are actually little cheese particles. That knowledge can be used to make a whole little cheese with lemon. It's the acid in the lemon that causes the casein in the milk to precipitate.

Mix 1 quart of milk with the juice of one lemon. Heat the milk until it is very warm but not boiling hot. When the milk starts to curdle, take the saucepan off the stove. Let it stand until the whey looks yellowish. If it doesn't turn yellow, heat it again and mix in more lemon juice. Drain the cheese in a sieve with a cloth. (The whey, which has a very good lemony taste, is good to drink when cooled and sweetened with honey.) If you can get unsprayed lemons, the grated lemon peel may be used to season the cheese further. This cheese is very tasty on dark rye bread.

Fresh Vinegar Cheese

Vinegar may also be used to make cheese; however, the cheese will taste vinegary and the whey cannot be used. I don't recommend this cheese, but find it interesting that any kind of acid may be used to make cheese. The milk for vinegar cheese should be lukewarm. Mix in the vinegar when the heating starts. I suggest a little test first to try the taste: ½ or 1 tablespoon of vinegar for ⅔ cup of milk.

Sour Cream Cheese

This is a really good rich cheese. Nobody could guess that it is made from sour cream, because it doesn't taste the least bit sour! Keep thick cream at room temperature until it sours. To hasten the process, a spoonful of curdled milk may be added. When the cream is sour, pour it directly into a cheesecloth or other type of cloth. Tie with a string and put the bag on a hook to drip. The next day, open the bag and work the cream cheese curds with a knife until they have a smooth consistency. Season with salt, cumin and strong grated cheese. Pack the cheese into a mold rinsed with water and turn it over onto a platter.

Gammalost

One of the oldest cheeses in Scandinavia, *gammalost*, is a brownish soft cheese made of sour milk. To give it the correct "old" taste, it is ripened from one to six months. For those who aren't used to it, it takes a lot of self-discipline to force down the first piece of this cheese. It really has a peculiar taste—or maybe one should be kind and call it "special." At any rate, in the old days it was not special. It was everyday food.

This sour gammalost is not at all like another so-called gammalost, which contains rennet. This is ordinary homemade sweet-milk cheese or skim-milk cheese that is left to ripen in the cellar until it practically crawls out by itself. It is described later in the section, "From Firm Rennet Cheese to 'Old' Cheese." The sour gammalost that we are talking about now is made in a completely different way. It looks more like a fresh cheese which has been left in a corner and forgotten.

In Norway this cheese is still being sold in grocery stores. Evidently there are people who like it, which seems incredible. But maybe the same thing can be said about French blue cheeses by those who haven't learned to appreciate their strong taste. Perhaps this cheese has not become known simply because it never was discovered by the gourmets at the courts of Europe in the Middle Ages! This cheese is actually Norway's own "Roquefort" cheese—it contains the *Pencillium roqueforti*.

As late as the 1960s, this cheese was made on Swedish mountain-dairy farms. Carefully skimmed milk was kept in wooden troughs until it became sour and thick. Then it was heated slowly in the cheese kettle. The portions were sizable—at least 50 liters. The curds separated from the whey, first during the souring and then still more during the heating. Then curds were poured into a round wooden bowl lined with a cheesecloth, which was tied around the cheese. Finally the whole bundle was boiled in the whey, half an hour on each side. The cloth was removed, and the cheese was left on a shelf to ripen. If it was very hot, the cheese ripened quickly—a month was probably enough. Then the cheese had turned soft and brown and acquired a strong smell.

Some old people say that this cheese should ripen in bedstraw, but I doubt that foam rubber mattresses would serve the purpose, so I think we might skip that.

Fifty liters is not an easy quantity to experiment with, so I started first with 2 quarts and then with 4. Just as with the naturally soured fresh cheese described earlier, it is easy until you get to the boiling. A small cheese like this gets boiled through too quickly. Cheeses weighing 4-8 pounds react entirely differently from those weighing 3½ ounces when they are boiled.

The first little cheese turned hard as a rock and became granular. With the second slightly larger cheese, instead of tying the cheesecloth, I held it open and let the cheese rest in it like in a hammock between my hands. Then I lowered it into the boiling whey, and when the edges of the cheese melted from the heat, I made it roll around so that it wouldn't get stuck in the cloth. From time to time, I picked it up so that it wouldn't get too hot all the way through. Thus this this cheese acquired a smooth surface, which a proper old cheese is not supposed to have. But on the other hand, this smooth rind actually tasted a little like the chewy boiled surface on an honest-to-goodness Norwegian gammalost. Inside the cheese was granular, as gammalost is supposed to be.

I placed my gammalost in a plastic jar with a lid to ripen on the windowsill in the living room. The heat from the radiator under the window warmed up the sill and hastened the ripening.

Flavoring of Fresh Cheeses

The soft fresh cheeses frequently need some extra spices to prevent them from tasting bland and are the easiest to mix with spices and various flavorings.

Experiment wildly with your seasoning: use whatever is handy. In the spring it might be chopped chives; in the summer, dill, parsley or other kinds of herbs; and in the fall, juniper berries. Watercress seeds can either be mixed into the curds or the finished cheese may be rolled in them.

Cumin is a common cheese spice, which is especially suitable for lemon cheese. Boiling water poured over the seeds will soften them and bring out the flavor. The lemon cheese may also be rolled in crushed coriander seeds. To emphasize the citrus taste, a tablespoon of orange concentrate may be added.

If a pepper cheese is desired, black pepper may be mixed with the cheese, and when ready the cheese may be rolled in the pepper corns until it gets black. Allspice adds a good but not so strong taste.

The cream cheese consists of sour cream which has been drained through a cheesecloth. The seasoning used was cumin and strong grated cheese. A dangerously delicious sandwich spread!

Solid fresh cheeses cut into slices taste good without special seasoning. However, try seasoning with green pepper or garlic. If green pepper is used, it should be mixed in with the cheese. Crushed garlic should be mixed with the curds, and chopped parsley may be rolled on the outside.

There is also walnut cheese with chopped walnuts mixed in and whole walnuts on top, curry cheese, cheese with paprika and cheese with brandy.

Fresh Cheese for Breakfast, Lunch and Dinner

Fresh cheese is good for sandwiches, both as a spread and cut in slices. Butter is not at all necessary; the cheese is rich enough. A good combination is a lettuce leaf, fresh cheese and sliced tomatoes or a slice of green pepper.

For dinner the fresh cheese may be the main source of protein. Add to it boiled potatoes, raw vegetables and a slice of bread and you have a wholesome meal. Or you can serve the cheese as dessert, with fruit and berries.

The spreadable fresh cheeses are good ingredients in all kinds of cooking. Russian and East European recipes often call for fresh cheeses with or without seasoning, as fillings in pies and other dishes.

Curds mixed with chocolate sauce make a delicious and nutritious filling for cakes. Another good filling may be made by mixing the fresh cheese with mashed bananas and cinnamon—both tastier and healthier than whipping cream.

Chapter 6

Hard Cheeses

Once you have made fresh cheese, you can see that it is not especially difficult to separate milk into curds and whey. For hard cheeses, rennet, or a vegetable enzyme, is used as a coagulating agent. Mixing rennet or vegetable enzyme in milk to make cheese is really no different from mixing yeast in dough to make bread.

Rennet tablets can be purchased in many drug, health, and grocery stores. Vegetable enzyme tablets may have to be ordered from one of the supply houses listed at the end of this book—Chr. Hansens and Dairyland Laboratories being definite sources. In fact, such sources may be your best bet for rennet, too, if you prefer to use that. With such supplies you will usually receive detailed instructions for use. Ask for them when you order.

Although it is not difficult to make the milk curdle, it *is* difficult to make a good-tasting cheese. It takes some practice before one can be assured of a consistently good result in cheesemaking. So don't be disappointed if the first cheeses sour, ferment, or split. That happens to even accomplished cheesemakers, and from each cheese, successful or not, you learn something.

Important factors that influence results are times and temperatures in the different stages of cheesemaking, cleanliness in the kitchen, the working of the curds, and such things as flavorings.

It takes time before a cheese is ready to eat. A cheese should not be cut until it is at least three weeks old, and it is preferable to be patient and wait a month, or better still, six weeks. Then the cheese is much tastier. If you like strong-tasting cheeses you should let them ripen up to six months in a cool place. But they have to be checked for molds from time to time.

The color of cheese, like the color of butter, differs at different times of the year, depending upon the fat content of the milk. The fatter the cheese, the more yellow it looks. In the winter cheese becomes yellow-white, but when the cows are out to pasture, the cheese may turn beautifully yellow. A ripened sheep cheese may turn completely yellow even if the sheep are still eating hay—sheep's milk has a higher fat content. The outside of the cheese is darker yellow than the inside. Dairies add food coloring to give cheese the same color the year around. If you make cheese at home you do not need to do that.

The recipes for hard rennet cheeses may be used with milk from various animals. Separate chapters in this book are devoted to sheep and goat cheese.

The first recipe couldn't be simpler. It comes from several different former mountain-dairy maids, who have told how they made cheese during many summers of hard work.

White Mountain-Dairy Cheese

Mountain-dairy cheese was of course made from nonpasteurized milk. Thus all bacteria (useful as well as harmful) were alive and multiplied as desired. But useful lactic bacteria have been destroyed in the pasteurized store-bought milk. If you were to strictly follow the mountain-dairy recipe, you would need access to nonpasteurized cow's milk directly from the barn.

White cheese is not only the easiest to make, it also has the simplest and least expensive ingredients. The mountain-dairy cheese was always made from skim milk, since the cream was used for making butter. Only when special cheeses were to be made was whole milk used—maybe for the Christmas cheese, which was made in late summer. But we might just as well make our cheese from ordinary sweet whole milk. It is, after all, easier to get a good-tasting cheese using whole milk than using skim milk.

Just like the mountain-dairy maid, we heat the milk slowly over low heat, until it becomes "udder-warm," about 98.6°F. Measure the temperature with a thermometer to be on the safe side. Stir the milk while it is being heated to make it uniformly warm.

Remove the saucepan from the heat and add the rennet, which you must first mix in *cold* water. The amount of water should be about three to four times the amount of rennet, for example 1 teaspoon to 1 tablespoon of water, so the rennet will mix more easily with the milk. The proportions of rennet, or vegetable enzyme, to the milk are usually given in instructions you will get with your rennet supply. Be sure to ask for them when you buy or order. The material varies in strength according to supplier. Add the rennet *im-*

Washed cheese drains and cheese troughs drying in the sun.

mediately after it is mixed with the water. Stir thoroughly but gently, so the rennet mixes properly, and then stop stirring to prevent the milk from moving while it curdles.

Cover with a lid or cloth so the surface doesn't cool off, and let the milk curdle for about an hour. Then press with a spoon against the surface of the curds. The whey should appear, and should be yellow and transparent. If it is whitish in color, curdling is not yet finished. If the curds float together when the spoon is lifted and stick to the bottom of the spoon, they are not ready. You may also put a finger or knife into the curds and raise them toward the surface to break them just above your finger. If the breaks are straight, whole and smooth, the curds are ready. If they are uneven and the whey is muddy from the cheese particles, the curdling should continue further.

When the curds are ready, they should be broken up. Use a long knife to cut them into uniform pieces, first horizontally and then vertically. After breaking the curds, the stirring should continue slowly, and any larger lumps that rise to the surface should be divided. Let the kettle stand for about 15 minutes and then remove the curds.

Line the cheese mold with a cheesecloth dipped in the warm whey. With clean hands lift the curds from the kettle and place them in the mold. When the mold is full, fold the cheesecloth over the cheese. Fold it as smoothly as possible, since all folds will be imprinted on the cheese. Press out with your hands as much whey as possible. A weight may be put on top.

After about an hour you may test to see if the cheese keeps together enough to be carefully taken out of the mold and then put back again upside down. Especially if a colander is used, the cheese should be turned over as soon as possible to give it a rounded shape on both sides.

The cheese may be taken out of the mold the next day, wrapped in a dry cloth and left to dry on a cutting board. It should be turned every day and care should be taken that it always rests on a dry surface. A long towel may be used, wrapping the cheese first with one side of the towel. When the cheese is turned, the other side is used, while the first side dries out. The cheese should be kept at room temperature the whole time. When the cheese is dry, it can not be infected by harmful bacteria. It is a good idea, however, to cover it with a cloth.

Put the cheese in a kitchen cupboard. Turn it once a week (more often the first few days) and leave it for up to six weeks. If mold appears, it may be washed off with a little salt water.

The difference between the old-fashioned mountain-dairy cheese and today's homemade cheeses is that the whey with the curds is not stirred as long after the breaking, and is heated only before the

Anna Wedin of Pipare mountain-dairy farm, is brushing her white cheese clean from mold, which has begun to appear.

rennet is added. This gives the cheese a higher whey content. The higher water content causes the cheese to age more rapidly and get its flavor more quickly.

Cheese from Öland

The following recipe comes from the island of Öland in the Baltic, off the Swedish coast. It may be describing one of the forerunners of what today's dairies call *prästost* (priest cheese). It is similar to priest cheese in the way it is salted and seasoned, and even has the same small irregularly shaped holes evenly distributed over the whole cheese.

To 10-12 quarts of milk add 1-2 tablespoons of cheese rennet. Heat the milk to between 80-100°F., add the rennet and let stand for half an hour. Break the curds, let stand 10 minutes, then strain and break the curds into very small pieces. Mix in a minimum of 1 tablespoon of table salt, ground ginger or cumin. Squeeze and press the mixture into a mold. Turn it over every couple of hours for the first day, then turn it every morning and night. Change the cloth twice a day for about eight days. Some people wash the cheese and rub it with aquavit or other alcohol to prevent it from molding. First it is ripened at 60-65°F., later at about 55-60°. The cheese needs to ripen for at least seven or eight weeks. This cheese ripens more quickly than the one in the earlier recipe because it is salted.

The leftover whey is made into a porridge by boiling it for a couple of hours, and then adding rice or corn meal to it. There is a sewing circle that has gotten together since the beginning of the 1950s to make this type of cheese, which they remember from their own childhood at the beginning of the 1900s. They use

Traditional cheese baskets and cheese molds. In the foreground a fresh cheese basket, braided from roots, an ordinary braided basket, and a goat cheese trough with dovetailed corners and carved bottom with drainage holes. In the background, is an old cheese trough held together with plugs. The little holes in the sides are difficult to keep clean and are not necessary for draining the whey. The trough doesn't have a bottom and is placed on top of a cheese drainer. The metal mold is an egg-cheese mold from southern Sweden. The wooden mold on its side is the one described in the section, "Tools for the Serious Cheesemaker."

braided rattan baskets as molds and sometimes store-bought tin molds.

Better Cheese through New Methods

One of the problems concerning older cheese recipes is that too much whey may remain in the cheese. In dairies the whey and curds are always slightly heated after breaking. Pre-stirring before the heating and post-stirring after the heating contributes to the draining of the whey from the cheese particles, which consequently become more solid. The longer the stirring and the hotter the whey, the more solid the cheese particles.

One way of testing is to taste the cheese particles. If they resist when you bite into them, the curds are ready to be shaped. The particles should feel solid and elastic. They are not all ready at the same time; there is a noticeable difference between the solid particles and the soft ones, which are shiny because of higher humidity content.

In the past the milk was curdled at a temperature of 98.6°F. for fast coagulating. In those days the rennet was weaker and of poorer quality, and thus such a high temperature was necessary. Now, with better rennet available, we may keep the curdling temperature at about 90°F. To reduce the amount of rennet and keep the temperature high would not be good, since the original amount of rennet is needed not only for the actual curdling, but also for proper ripening of the cheese. Another disadvantage of fast curdling at a high temperature is that it is harder to stop the curdling at the right moment. At a lower temperature it is easier to follow the change in the milk and start breaking the curds at the right moment.

In the old days people also kept a high curdling temperature because the cheese was often made in wash houses or in other chilly places where the milk quickly cooled. Today in dairies and ordinary kitchens the temperature is kept at a level that is more pleasant for people, cheeses and curdling milk.

Modern Homemade Cheese

By using the knowledge and experience of the dairy industry it is becoming easier to produce better homemade cheeses. It is slightly more involved than the old way, but your chances of success are greater. The following recipe for a homemade cheese is a variation of a dairy cheese. Ripening is called for in this recipe.

Start the day before the actual cheesemaking by preparing an acid culture which will control the bacteria growth in the cheese to be made.

For 10 quarts of milk, boil ½ cup of milk and cool to 70°F. Mix it with 1 tablespoon of curdled milk and let stand at a temperature of between 65-70°F. until the following day. If more than 10 quarts is desired, increase the amount of curdled milk proportionately.

On the day the cheese is to be made, the milk is heated to 85°F. and the acid culture, which now has become thick, is added. After 20 minutes, check that the milk still has a temperature of 85°F. Dilute 1 tablespoon of commercial rennet in three times as much cold water and mix immediately into the kettle with the milk. The diluted rennet deteriorates rapidly if left to stand. Stir so that the rennet is properly mixed, and then stop the milk from swirling. Cover the milk with a lid or cloth so it doesn't cool off too quickly.

After 35 minutes to an hour the curdling is finished. Clear whey should become visible at the edges of the saucepan, and the breaks in the curds should be smooth and shiny. The curds are now ready for cutting.

It is important to cut the curds carefully so that smooth and even pieces are obtained instead of loose cheese particles, mixed with the whey. Cut carefully with a long knife, first horizontally, into long standing slices. Then cut across the slices vertically, so that the result will be square "poles" of curds standing in the kettle. Finally cut the poles into cubes, slightly smaller than sugar cubes. This may be accomplished either by cutting across, first from the left to the right and then from the right to the left, or you may carefully turn the poles with clean hands or two spoons so that they lie down and are easier to cut. The cubes of cheese should be uniform in size.

Dividing the curds into small pieces makes the separation of the whey from the cheese particles easier. The whey oozes out, and if the pieces of curds are of the same size, all the cheese particles are drained at the same time. Stir carefully from the bottom up, in order to keep the pieces floating in the whey, instead of forming lumps at the bottom. Care must be taken at the beginning of the stirring to prevent the curds from becoming granular and mixing with the whey.

After 10 minutes of stirring, the curds and whey are heated very slowly, at the rate of about 5 degrees' increase every 5 minutes. If the curds are heated too quickly, the surface of the cheese particles closes, and the whey inside can not ooze out. At the same time, stir vigorously (now that the risk of the curds mixing with the whey is smaller), to prevent the cheese from settling on the warm bottom of the kettle.

Heat to about 100°F. The higher the temperature, the lower the water content of the cheese. Cheese with a higher fat content is heated at a higher temperature than cheese with a lower fat content.

After heating, the stirring continues until the cheese particles are solid and have the right consistency. Squeeze a few of the curds in your hand. Let go and see if the curds expand, or "bounce back," after having been squeezed. If so, the cheese particles are ready. If not, you will have to stir longer, anywhere from 15 minutes to an hour.

The molding is done differently for different cheeses.

Priest cheese (*prästosten*), which is meant to be granular, is placed in a large colander; the curds are cut into small pieces and mixed with salt (½ ounce for 10 quarts of milk). They are then placed in a mold lined with a warm cloth dipped in whey, and a weight is put on top. Granular cheese is ripened at room temperature.

Manor cheese (*Herrgärdsosten*) is not salted while being made. The curds must be gathered from under the whey in order to prevent air from getting between the cheese particles when the cheese is formed. Lactic bacteria form carbon dioxide, which causes the large holes so typical of manor cheese.

Keep a large cheesecloth handy near the kettle. Stir clockwise with a wooden spoon. This causes the curds to form in the middle of the kettle and makes it easier to collect the particles with the cloth. Hold the cloth as close to the edge of the kettle as possible. Keep the cloth stretched between your hands and move your hands along the side of the kettle, down toward the bottom, along the bottom and then up the other side, collecting most of the curds in the cloth. Bring the edges of the cloth together to form a bundle, while still keeping it below the surface of the whey. Twist the bundle together so that the whey is pressed out of the cloth, and place it in the cheese mold. Once in the mold, the bundle may be opened, and the cloth wrapped smoothly around the cheese. A weight is put on top, and the cheese is turned as often as necessary to give it an even shape. This means about every 4 hours for the first 24 hours, after which the weight may be removed.

When a cheese with big holes is dried, it may be salted, and is then stored in a cool place for a couple of weeks, and at room temperature later.

Watch the cheese carefully when you are about to take it out of the mold. If it shows signs of collapsing, it must remain in the mold longer. A round cheese that is molded in a sieve should remain longer in the sieve so as not to become flat. Since the sieve is ventilated, the surface of the cheese dries well all around.

The cheese should be protected from getting cooled while in the mold. If the mold is made of wood there is no danger. Plastic and metal molds, however, should be kept warm, either by keeping them in a warm place or by wrapping cloths around them.

Surface Treatment of Hard Cheese

No special surface treatment is necessary in most cases. As long as the cheese dries reasonably fast, a rind will develop that protects it against mold. However, you must take care that the cheese is not drying out too much. The easiest and least dangerous way to prevent this is to rub the cheese with oil or salted butter. This should be done only when the surface of the cheese is completely dry. To prevent the cheese from getting too hard, it may be washed with lukewarm water from time to time. The surface must not be constantly damp, however, so as not to encourage the growth of mold. Any kind of alcohol may be used to wash the cheese to prevent it from molding.

If the cheese cracks after its surface has dried, pieces of butter may be used to fit into the cracks to prevent bugs from getting into the cheese. If butter is used, the cheese should be kept at a lower temperature in order to prevent the butter from turning rancid before the cheese is ready. Unless there is reason for avoiding salty food, the cheese may be put into a salt solution to give it a solid surface. In the summer especially, when higher temperatures cause the bacteria to flourish, it might be a good idea to salt the cheese on the outside. Put a few handfuls of salt in a bucket of water and stir. There should be just enough for a raw potato to be able to float! When the salt doesn't dissolve any more but stays on the bottom, the solution is saturated. Keep the cheese in the solution overnight, in not too warm a place. Put some salt on the part of the cheese that remains above the solution. The solution may be used for a long time, for many cheeses. If it turns yellow and slimy, all you have to do is boil it again to make it clear.

The surface of the cheese may also be salted dry, by simply sprinkling it with salt. This way is more suitable for soft cheeses, such as blue cheese, since the growth of the mold culture would otherwise be impeded.

The surface of the cheese may also be waxed or covered with paraffin, but those methods are too complicated for the amateur cheesemaker. If the cheese is carefully watched, its surface should require no complicated treatment.

Port Salut

Treating the cheese with a salt solution creates a suitable environment for the kind of bacteria which gives Port Salut its typical orange rind. The rind is not just for looks, but also gives a special smell and taste to the cheese. With the aid of bacteria, the cheese doesn't ripen from the inside as do other cheeses, but from the outside, and therefore this cheese is made fairly flat.

The rind in homemade Port Salut, unlike most rinds, is eaten. Modern Port Salut cheese made in dairies has food coloring added to the surface of the rind to give an orange-red color. I would suggest cutting off the rind in this case, for you will not lose any of the flavor.

To make Port Salut we may treat our cheese approximately the same way. Make a flat cheese, about 2½ inches high. When the cheese has solidified, put it in a salt solution for 24 hours. The salt solution should be strong enough for a potato to float in it.

Store the cheese for ripening at about 65°F. in a place where the air is humid. The cheese should be placed so that air can circulate all around it. Brush the cheese every day with a cool, weak salt solution made by boiling half a teaspoon of salt with half a quart of water, and let it cool. As long as the surface is not affected by the wrong kind of bacteria, brush and turn the cheese every day. If the cheese seems to be adversely affected by frequent brushing, stop for a couple of days. When the cheese has turned the right reddish color, it will take only three to four weeks before it is ready. But even after 10-14 days it starts to develop a certain aroma.

Ripening of Hard Cheese

In the old days cellars in the ground were perfect for storing cheese while ripening since the humidity there was just right, except during the coldest winter months.

Nowadays, ground cellars are not readily available, but that doesn't mean poorer quality cheese. The cheese will quickly ripen in ordinary room temperature. After a while it may be placed in a cooler pantry if the room temperature seems to be too warm. Cheeses which must ripen many months should be kept cooler than those with a shorter ripening time. If the air is very dry, the cheese will become dry too, and develop a thicker rind. This may be prevented by dampening the cheese a little from time to time.

One cheesemaker I know pours water over bricks to achieve the proper humidity in his cheese cupboard—a good idea! Again, what I am stressing is if you watch your cheese closely you will be able to prevent loss due to mold, cracking or drying out too quickly.

From Firm Rennet Cheese to "Old" Cheese

A cheese with multicolored molds and an almost liquid consistency may cause the right person to fall into ecstasy. An honest-to-goodness "old" cheese!

Other people may turn up their noses and mutter about worms and air pollution.

In the old days there were many tricks to aging and perfecting ordinary hard cheese. Placing the cheese in a manure pile supposedly gave it the proper environment and heat. I know of a person who tried it, but a fox found the cheese and ate it!

Another method was digging a hole in the ground, lining it with leaves and putting the cheese into it. If the cheese was stored in a ground cellar, leaves were also used. Layers of cheeses were alternated with layers of leaves in a box. In one to two weeks the cheeses were ripe. The leaves kept the cheeses warm and thus facilitated their ripening. Gray alder leaves were often used for this purpose, particularly in the northern part of Sweden where that tree is common, and the tradition began for using leaves for storing and ripening cheese. In southern Europe and the Mediterranean, cheese wrapped in grape leaves is common.

From Stine Larsson in Bjuräker, a village in northern Sweden, comes this description of how her mother made "old" cheese. The description is easy enough for us to try.

First the cheese was made as usual. When the milk had curdled, the curds were stirred for a short while until they turned granular. The whey was poured off and the curds were put into a cheese mold lined with a cheesecloth. The cheese was squeezed, then turned and squeezed again. The rest of the whey drained through the cheese drainer. The next day the cheese was taken out of the mold and unwrapped. It was then left for 12 hours in a salt solution made from a bucket of water and one handful of salt. This gave it a strong and smooth surface. It was left to dry on a shelf and turned every day.

Then a juniper solution was made for the cheese by boiling a couple of juniper twigs with berries for a few minutes. The solution was strained and cooled, and a handful of salt was added. The cheese was placed in the juniper solution for a couple of days to make it yellow and pretty. It was then removed and left to dry again for another week. When dry it was rubbed with a mixture of mes-butter (made from whey) and molasses. (The molasses prevented the mes from drying.) This mixture kept the cheese soft. Again the cheese was left for a week on a shelf, and was turned every day and even sometimes put on its side. Finally it was kept in the ground cellar, in a wooden box with a lid. It was ready after about a month.

Imperfections and Remedies

Each time you make a cheese you begin to gather experience and it becomes easier to know when the cheese is a success and when it is not. The cheese seldom is such a failure that it is inedible. There are a few tips, however, which may help you improve your cheesemaking.

One of the most difficult things is preventing cheese from becoming sour. Dairymen consider a sour cheese the worst thing there is. But I have also heard people who make cheese at home say that they would rather have a sour cheese than a fermented one that is completely inedible. A sour cheese is at least fresh!

Here are a few tips:

Hard and sour cheese is the result of too short a curdling time.

Tough and dry cheese is the result of too long a curdling time.

The important thing is to find a happy medium. If the cheese turns out *sour*, the curds should be broken into smaller cubes, so the whey can drain from them more quickly. In addition, the post-warming temperature should be higher and the post-stirring time longer.

If the cheese *ferments after only a few days*, it may be infected by bacteria, especially if untreated cow's milk was used. Then a checkup of overall cleanliness is in order.

If the cheese *ferments after a couple of weeks*, the fermentation may be stopped by putting the cheese in a cooler place.

If the *surface of the cheese cracks*, and fermentation is not the cause, it may be because the cheesecloths were not warm enough when the cheese was molded. It is important to make the cheese particles cohesive and form a smooth even surface. This problem is the greatest when granular cheese is made, since air enters between the cheese particles. Cheese with holes formed below the surface of the whey is easier to keep smooth and free from cracks. A turkish towel that prevents heat from escaping may be used to cover the mold. If a heavy weight is put on the granular cheese, cracks are less apt to occur.

If the cheese *loses its shape* and is liquid when taken out of the mold, too little souring agent has been added.

A hard and solid cheese that doesn't change its shape at all is the result of too much souring agent. If the cheese is only slightly deformed when taken out of the mold, the acid content is just right. It should become stabilized after about 24 hours.

Poorly coagulated curds and whitish whey are the result of curdling pasteurized milk without a souring agent. If this is the case, the curdling temperature should be increased to 99°F. and the milk should be left to curdle until it solidifies. Cut the curds into very small pieces. The post-heating temperature may be increased to 100°F. to facilitate the drying of the cheese particles.

Chapter 7

Soft Cheeses

The soft cheeses are often called dessert cheeses. To this group belong all the well-known foreign cheeses, like Camembert, Brie, Gorgonzola and many others. (These soft cheeses should not be confused with what the Swedes often call *mjukost*, which is another type of soft cheese often mixed with mushrooms, shrimp, etc., and used as a spread on bread. These kinds of cheese should be called "smelt cheeses," since they are made often from melted cheese.)

Soft cheeses are made the same way as the hard rennet cheeses to begin with. But in order to make them soft and more liquid, whey must remain in the cheese. Thus the curds are broken just a little, or not at all. They are carefully placed in molds, from which the whey drains. Seasoning often consists of adding a mold culture (fungi) in the form of a powder or solution. The cheese is then stored in surroundings favorable to the growth of mold. The purpose of the mold is not only to give taste, but also to give some cheeses their buttery, soft consistency.

Mold cheeses are not difficult to make. The taste is easily achieved—if not exactly like the original, at least a fair imitation. The structure and appearance of the cheese is harder to copy. But as usual, practice makes perfect.

Soft Dessert Cheese

The first description is of a soft cheese without mold culture. It is the basic recipe, which may be varied by adding different types of mold cultures and seasonings.

If the cheese is to be made from store-bought milk, start the day before the actual cheesemaking by preparing the souring agent. That won't be necessary if untreated milk is used, but it might be a good idea if the quality of the cheese is in doubt.

The amount of milk used depends upon the molds available. Ten quarts of milk will yield one large cheese the size of a cake, and several little ones. If there are curds left over, for variety you may use them for making cottage cheese. Three quarts of milk will yield six cheeses 2½ inches in diameter.

Day one: The procedure is the same as for hard cheese. After the milk has ripened (see the section, "Cultures to 'Ripen' the Milk"), the milk must be kept at curdling temperature, 90°F. Add rennet dissolved in three times its amount of cold water; 1 tablespoon of the rennet solution for 10 quarts of milk, or 1 teaspon for three quarts of milk. Let the milk curdle in the saucepan covered with a lid for at least 1 hour.

In the meantime, the utensils for the molding of the cheeses should be prepared. Boil the molds for a few minutes, and let them dry in the air. Prepare cheese-cloths, draining board and other utensils needed. (See the section, "Tools for Cheesemaking.")

Test to see if the curdling is finished in the same manner as for hard cheeses.

Now comes the most important difference between the soft cheeses and hard cheese. Do not break the curds, but ladle them in layers directly from the sauce-pan carefully into the mold. The mold should be placed on a drainage mat, on top of a drain board in a bowl, or on a tray where the whey can be collected. Read about the utensils for the making of soft cheeses in the "Tools" section, and look at the accompanying photo-graphs there.

If the mold is lightweight and without a bottom, it must be supported in place with one hand. If not, the pressure from the curds will lift the mold, and the curd will overflow. This is particularly important when plas-tic and tin molds are used without a cheesecloth. A weight that is used only to keep the mold in place during draining should be kept handy, since you must put it on top immediately without letting go of the mold.

If the mold is high and narrow, a spoon or ladle with a 90-degree handle is desirable to reach the bottom of the mold without dropping curds.

Larger soft cheeses should be molded with a cloth between curds and the mold. Otherwise the surface of the cheese becomes too smooth, making it difficult for

A pressed garlic clove gives a strong taste to the mild curds. Alternately place layers of garlic and layers of curds, and let the whey drain. When the cheese is firm (after a couple of days) it is left to ripen in a cool place for about a week.

the whey to drain easily from the cheese. It is preferable to use cheesecloths even for smaller cheeses, but it is not as necessary.

Place the whole apparatus, including mold, weight (which must not press directly on the curds but is used only to keep the mold in place), drain board and whey collector in a warm place, so that the curds don't get chilled. If the molds are of the kind that easily get cold, extra care must be taken to place them in a warm place. Perhaps the whole apparatus should be covered with cloth.

Day two: Let the cheeses stand until the second day. Then the molds should be carefully turned upside down. Care must be taken not to break the cheeses. Slowly unwrap the cloth or drainage mat, in case the cheese is stuck to it. Wrap the cheese in a new cloth or put it on a new, dry drainage mat. Leave it set until the next day.

Day three: The third day the cheeses are usually firm enough to be removed from the molds. But watch the cheese carefully when it is taken out of the mold. If it begins to collapse it must be put back into the mold again until it has become firm enough.

If the cheese is not supposed to have any special mold on the outside, you may rub a little salt into it. Keep the cheese in a cool place or in the refrigerator. After a week it is ready to eat. The cheese may be stored in a cool place for a couple of weeks, but it doesn't improve by being ripened longer.

This cheese has a somewhat sour taste, since it contains a lot of whey and doesn't go through the process of post-heating. However, if added mold is to grow, the cheese should be sour, since mold thrives in a sour environment.

If a firmer cheese than the one just described is desired, the curds may be carefully broken in the saucepan to liberate the whey. That is how Roquefort cheese is made, for instance. The cheese is not post-heated, but the curds are broken in fairly big pieces and are left to drain in cheesecloth before being placed in molds.

Variations on the Basic Recipe

The curds may be mixed with all kinds of different seasonings, such as chopped walnuts, various chopped herbs, cumin, allspice, garlic or green pepper. They may also be wrapped in fragrant black currant or hop leaves. The leaves should be dipped into boiling water and tied around the cheese with a string.

Among all the different variations to be tried, the blue cheeses (or mold cheeses) are a must. The easiest way to make them is to buy a small piece of blue cheese in the store, and alternate it with layers of curds when the cheese is put into the molds. Or you may rub the inside of the molds with the mold. The strongest and easiest mold to work with is the green mold, *Penicillium roqueforti*. It reproduces easily and makes a fine cheese. White molds are weaker, but can also be cultivated. If you mix the green and the white, the green will prevail. Blue cheeses which have matured should be kept cold and wrapped in foil or a plastic wrap.

Green Cultured Cheese

The genuine green cultured cheese called Roquefort must be manufactured solely from sheep's milk and stored to maturity in the caves of Roquefort in France to be allowed to bear that label. That is why the

Swedish variety is called *ädelost* (noble cheese). There are many other kinds of blue cheese on the market, most of them made from cow's milk.

The genuine French blue cheese curdles at 85°F. Leave the milk to curdle for a long time, two hours or more. Cut the curds into pieces about ¾ inch in diameter, and leave them to drain for a while in a cheesecloth. A large colander lined with a cloth may be used, or else simply scoop the curds with a perforated ladle directly from the saucepan into the mold. Alternate layers of mold culture with layers of curds in the mold, which is lined with a cheesecloth dipped in the lukewarm whey. Or if the curds have been drained first in a colander, the culture may then be mixed in carefully. It is preferable to use concentrated mold dissolved in water.

The amount of mold culture used is small. For the cheese in the photograph in this section, only $^1/_5$ teaspoon (.03 ounce) of concentrated mold culture was used. It was dissolved in lukewarm whey in order to mix it more easily with the curds.

After an hour, or whenever feasible without the cheese falling apart, turn it upside down. Dip the cloth in the lukewarm whey again so that the cheese doesn't get chilled.

The cheese should be left in the mold until it is firm, and then wrapped in a cloth without a mold. It should be frequently turned, and kept at a temperature of about 65°F. In a couple of days it will be dry and may be easily handled.

Roquefort cheese is manufactured not only in the village with that name, but in several dairies in the area. But after being stored at 65°F. those cheeses are transported to Roquefort for further ripening. There they are kept for six days at a temperature of 50°F. and are salted with dry salt on the outside. When homemade blue cheese is made from sheep's milk in Sweden, the cheese is salted earlier, on the second day as well as the sixth day.

After being salted, the cheese is pricked to make holes in it to let in the air necessary for mold cultures to grow. A 5-inch nail may be used to make holes of just the right size to assure a constant supply of air.

The cheese is then kept at a temperature of about 40°F. The air should be as damp as possible. The caves of Roquefort have many crevices where rainwater collects, which makes the circulating air damp. Therein lies the secret of the exquisite blue cheese—proper temperature *and* humidity while ripening. A blue cheese is ready after about 2-3 months. Keep it in the refrigerator and eat it before it gets too old.

White Cultured Cheeses

Camembert mold, *Penicillium camemberti*, is used for white cultured cheeses. The mold culture may be bought in concentrated form or the mold from a Camembert or Brie cheese may be used. The white mold is also called *Penicillium candidum*, which is Latin for "white-shimmering brush." Magnified, the mold looks like a brush, and thus it is called brush mold. There are many different kinds of brush mold in addition to this one.

The warmer the kitchen, the better the mold develops and the whey drains. Ripen the milk with an acid culture as before. If cow's milk from the barn is used, it may be left overnight to ripen on its own. The curdling temperature should be 90°F. The time varies:

in France 1-1½ hours are needed, in Sweden 2-3 hours. Presumably, stronger rennet is added for the shorter curdling time.

The curds are molded without breaking. The mold culture may be added by rubbing the insides of the molds with the culture. The cheese may also be brushed with a mold solution when taken out of the mold. The outside may be salted either with dry salt or with a salt solution for a short while (1½ hours), but this is not mandatory.

The ripening should take place in a damp room. The first few days the cheese should be kept warm, but then the temperature should be lowered to about 60°F. It should be frequently turned. Soon white mold will appear on the outside. After 10-14 days the mold is fully developed and the cheese is wrapped in foil and kept in the coldest place in the refrigerator. Before the cheese is to be eaten, it is left for a day at room temperature.

Gorgonzola

This cheese originated in the village of Gorgonzola in the Po valley of northern Italy. It is reddish on the outside and white or yellow with green mold on the inside.

Stracchino di Gorgonzola is the full original name of this cheese. Stracchino means "tired" in Italian. The cheese was made from the milk of cows that returned in the fall from the mountain pastures to farms in the valley. The cows were naturally tired after their long walk, and so the cheese made from their milk got the name "tired from Gorgonzola!"

Whole milk is used for Gorgonzola. Start in the evening with half the amount of milk that will ultimately be used. Add slightly more rennet than usual. After about a quarter of an hour the curds are broken and left in the saucepan overnight.

On the second day curdle more milk in the same way. The curds are broken after 15 minutes, and left to drain in a colander for about a quarter of an hour. The cold and the lukewarm curds are now alternately layered in the molds, with lukewarm curds at the bottom and on top. At the same time add the mold culture. A piece of store-bought Gorgonzola, dissolved in a little lukewarm whey, may be used to make the mold culture. Let the cheese stand for a while, as usual, then turn it, and finally remove from the molds when feasible. This will take a few days at room temperature. Salt the cheese on the outside, and let it mature at a humid temperature of 50° to 60°F. for 2-3 months.

Fresh Cottage Cheese

Cottage cheese is the model for the fresh cheese that Swedish dairies call *Keso*. It contains very little acid, and therefore has a very mild taste—some people would say bland. Keso is granular, and is not easy to spread—it is preferably eaten with a spoon. Keso is used as a protein in vegetable dishes and is mixed in bread and pastry dough.

It is not difficult to make Keso at home, but it takes a little longer than making ordinary curdled-milk cheese. The following are needed: skimmed milk, rennet, a little curdled milk, salt and cream. This cheese will take a couple of hours before it is ready, but your actual working time is much less.

The milk must ripen or sour a little. This is done

either by starting the day before (see the section, "Cultures to Ripen the Milk") or on the same day. First heat the skim milk to room temperature and mix it with curdled milk, also at room temperature; 1 tablespoon for three quarts of milk, or 1 teaspoon for two quarts of milk. Let stand for an hour or a little longer.

Heat again to about 85°F. and mix in the rennet dissolved in water. One teaspoon of rennet and 3 teaspoons of water are enough for three quarts of milk. Let stand again until the milk has congealed. This takes about an hour.

Dairies use considerably less rennet, and it takes their milk almost 24 hours to coagulate. In this book I have shortened the time, but each cheesemaker may choose the way that suits him best.

Break the curds by cutting them into little cubes and stir for a few minutes. Heat slowly to 120°F. while stirring. Pour the curds into a sieve, placed over a bowl for the whey to drip into, and let drain. Separate them from time to time with your fingers, so that they don't get lumpy.

After an hour or so, the curds will be finished draining, with no more whey dripping into the bowl underneath. Crumble the curds again with your fingers, and mix in a dash of salt. Taste it! Put the curds into a jar and mix in a couple of spoonfuls of cream.

The salt and cream are optional. The whey may be put to good use for making mes or baking.

A speedy variety of Keso results if the post-heating process is skipped. Instead the curds are left in the whey for a while, poured and left to drain. This Keso too is perfectly acceptable.

Käsmus (Kiessmus or Tjesmus)

It is hard to decide how to spell a word which is usually only spoken and hardly ever written. But from the various alternatives one can at least get an idea on how to pronounce it.

Käsmus is quite simply fresh curds eaten as they are. While cheese is being made, a part of the cheese which has formed after curdling and stirring is put on a plate and served with cream. That is genuine mountain-dairy food! *Käs* or *tjes* is obviously related to the German *Käse* and the English *cheese*, and means the same thing.

Fresh Cheese Prepared on a Plate

Similar to *Käsmus* is the following dish, where the milk curdles right on the plate from which it is eaten. This cheese dish was formerly eaten for Sunday breakfast and considered a little better than ordinary porridge. It was quickly prepared from the warm morning milk, straight from the barn, so there was no need to heat the milk to reach the curdling temperature.

We must instead heat a little milk in a saucepan. Mix in a tiny bit of rennet and keep the mixture on a plate until whey appears at the edge of the plate. Whip it and pour off most of the whey. Pour cream over it and sprinkle with sugar.

Coffee Cheese from Arvidsjaur

From Lapland and probably originally from the Lap culture comes the tradition of putting cheese in coffee. When the reindeer cows were milked, it was customary to pour the milk into a rennet bag. When the milk had

turned to cheese it was used instead of cream in coffee
or coffee-like drinks.

Deep in the provinces of Norrbotten and Västerbot-
ten and in Lapland in northern Sweden, coffee cheese
is still considered a delicacy to be served at parties in
the countryside. On the coffee table is placed a bowl
with cheese cubes among the sugar and the cookies
and cake. The coffee is also served with cream for those
who wish it in addition to the cheese cubes. When the
coffee is drunk, the cheese, which has become warm
and tough from the coffee, is eaten. "A delicacy," says
Brita Grahn from the town of Arvidsjaur in Lapland. She
uses traditional cheese baskets braided from roots to
mold the cheeses and drain the whey. The recipe:

Seven quarts of whole milk are heated to about
98.6°F. If only store-bought milk is available, a little
cream may be mixed in to make it more like cow's milk.
Mix in a teaspoon of rennet. After about 25 minutes the
milk should be curdled. Heat lightly and stir so that the
whey separates. It must be no hotter than lukewarm.
Remove the curds with a perforated ladle and place in
cheese baskets. If no cheese baskets are available, a
colander or a large sieve may be used. Let the whey
drain off into a bowl, but don't press the curds. When
the whey has stopped dripping the cheese is put on a
platter and cut into pieces to put in the coffee.

Brita uses the sweetish whey when baking bread.
She maintains that it makes her dough rise particularly
well.

Coffee Cheese from Kuoksu

A slightly different, very old recipe for coffee cheese
comes from the county of Kiruna in northern Sweden.

Baskets for making coffee cheese—the kind that, in Sweden, is cut into cubes and put into coffee or coffee-like drinks. The cheeses are turned upside down onto plates. You see them in the background, with decorative patterns imprinted in them by the baskets.

The main difference in this recipe is that the cheese is baked in the oven before it is put in the coffee.

Eight to ten quarts of milk (cow's milk or regular milk mixed with cream) are heated until lukewarm. A tablespoon of rennet is mixed with the milk, and it is left to coagulate. Continue to stir from time to time while the milk gets firmer. Keep it on low heat, and press the curds a little as the whey is forming. Turn on the oven to 350° to 375°F.

Put a kettle lid (which can resist oven temperatures) upside down on a drip pan, and place the cheese in the lid. Press the cheese with a perforated ladle from time to time so that more whey drains. The cheese is supposed to get a light-brown crust on top, and is ready after about half an hour. Some makers of coffee cheese bake the other side of the cheese as well.

The cheese has now spread out into a cake less than an inch thick. What is to be used immediately is cut into pieces the size of sugar lumps and put into a bowl. The rest may be frozen.

One detail in the recipe may seem strange, namely the use of a lid as a mold for the cheese. In an ordinary mold with edges the cheese would not be able to spread out properly, and neither would the whey drain. It is not possible to put the cheese on an ordinary grill, since the cheese would slip through the bars. A net on a frame or a flat perforated dish would be ideal—but are unavailable unless you make them yourself. So until something better is found, an upside-down lid will have to do.

Bread Cheese from East Bothnia

East Bothnia is the Finnish province that follows the bay of Bothnia from the Swedish border in the north to the same parallel as the town of Sundsvall on the Swedish side. Here both "Finlanders" and Finns live— Finns with Swedish and Finnish as their native tongues respectively. In Finnish the bread cheese is called *Peräpohjalainen leipäjuusto* (*juusto* means cheese). Bread cheese is often served at coffee parties in Finnish families. Similar baked cheeses are called *stekost* (fried cheese) or *bryntost* (sautéed cheese) in Sweden.

Eight quarts of milk with some cream added are heated to 98.6°F. Add 1 tablespoon of salt and 1 tablespoon of rennet and let the milk curdle. Stir to make the whey drain from the coagulating curds. Place the curds on an upside-down lid and flatten carefully with a ladle. But don't press them. The mixture is supposed to take the shape of a flat cake by itself. When the whey has drained from the cheese it should be broiled in the oven on both sides. The oven should be hot enough for the cheese to be broiled brown on the surface. It mustn't be baked all the way through, which would be the case if it were left on low heat for a long time.

If the milk gets too hot when the rennet is added, or if the cheese is baked rather than broiled, the bread cheese turns out squeaky. In spite of all precautions it sometimes happens that the cheese becomes tough. The cheese is served cut in squares, carefully placed on a platter.

Cheesecake from Hälsingland

Bertil Bylin, from Tomsjö village in the province of Hälsingland in northern Sweden, milks his ten goats and two cows by hand. From the goat milk he makes goat cheese and mes, but from the cow's milk he makes cheesecakes, which he sells in the neighborhood grocery store. As a transition between the receipes for cheese dishes and cheesecakes, his recipe is an apt one. His cheesecake is different from others in that it is made from only milk and rennet, and thus is similar to coffee cheese and bread cheese.

Cheesecake without eggs is an old mountain-dairy tradition, originally called sållost (sieve cheese), since the curds were placed in a sieve for draining before being put in the oven. Chickens were not kept at the mountain-dairy, and consequently eggs were not included in the diet.

Heat 10 quarts of milk to 98.6°F. Mix 2 tablespoons of commercial rennet with the milk and leave for half an hour to coagulate. The proportions may be halved, if the above seems to be too much.

Cut the curds into pieces of about 4 inches, but don't stir. Place the saucepan in a cool place for at least an hour so that the whey separates. If the place is cool enough, the cheese may be left longer.

Pour the curds into a colander and let them drain. Don't pour the mixture back and forth, since this may result in a tough and rubbery cheese. Just pour the curds directly from the saucepan into the colander. After at least a half hour the curds are placed in an ungreased 3-quart mold. The mold should be heaped with the curds so that the whey which drains during the baking overflows the edge of the mold. Place the mold in a drip pan. When the whey runs over the edges down into the drip pan, the cheesecake is not only baked from above but is also boiled in a waterbath. If the mold is too big or the amount of curds too small, water may be added to the drip pan to create a waterbath. Then the whey has to be scooped out of the mold as it separates.

Bake at about 300°F. for an hour and a half, or until the cheesecake is brownish-yellow on top. It may get this color before it is baked through. This problem may be avoided by placing a cookie sheet over the cheesecake in the oven, and then removing it after about 45 minutes. Some recipes call for the removal of the brown crust, and baking again until the cake forms a new crust. But this of course means that a good portion of the cake is wasted.

If the cake is not to be eaten within a couple of days, it should be kept in the freezer. When it is taken out of the freezer, place it in a mold, pour a little milk or cream over it, and put it in the oven at 400°F. When the milk around the cake is boiling, the cake has been heated through. This way a certain grainy quality sometimes caused by freezing is avoided.

A Different Cheesecake from Hälsingland

Recipes for cheesecake vary not only among the various provinces, but also between villages. The reason for this is mainly the different standards of living on different farms. In poor villages cheesecake was made with less expensive ingredients than in the wealthier areas. The cheesecake from the province of Småland in southern Sweden is richer than the one from Hälsingland in northern Sweden. But even in the one from Hälsingland, eggs may be included, as in the following recipe. This cheesecake is a little fancier and richer. This recipe is different from most others in that the proportions are just right for one family. Our friend Stina Larsson in Bjuråker uses this recipe from time to time:

Heat 4 quarts of milk and add 4 or 5 sugar lumps and 1 tablespoon of rennet. Stir very slowly with a wooden whisk while the milk is curdling until whey begins to form. Remove the whisk and shake out the cheese stuck to it. Pour off the whey, but don't press on the curds, or they will turn hard.

Whisk together exactly 4 tablespoons of wheat flour with a little cold milk and 2 eggs, and mix with the curds. Bake the cheesecake in a mold large enough to prevent the whey from dripping over the edge. The heat should be about 350°F., hot enough for the whey to boil rapidly. If it takes too long, the cheesecake will be tough. Open from time to time and scoop whey from the mold. Leave some whey, however, in which to boil the cake.

This cheesecake may be eaten warm or cold. If desired, it may be heated before serving, cut into slices and put on a platter with openings between the slices. Pour cream on top so that it fills the openings. Cold berry sauce is often served with warm cheesecake, as well as preserves or fresh berries. There are no spices in this cheesecake, but a little cinnamon may be sprinkled over the cake when it is ready.

Genuine Cheesecake from Småland

Any cheesecake from the province of Småland in southern Sweden is usually described as "genuine." Of all the cheesecakes described in this book, this is the most expensive and richest—although it may of course be simplified when one can't afford to use such a large number of eggs for a cake. Hence the need to distinguish between the less rich cheesecakes and the "genuine" one from Småland—but the cheesecakes from other Swedish provinces are just as genuine!

A delicious cheesecake which even the novice cheesecake eater will find eminently edible comes from the village of Krisdale near the town of Lskarshamn in the province of Småland. Compared to other cheesecake recipes, it contains a little less sugar, flour and cream, but still enough to be dangerously delicious. It is not a cake for people on a diet.

Ten quarts of milk are heated to 98.6°F. and the saucepan is removed from the stove. Mix 7 tablespoons of wheat flour with a half a quart of milk, stir so the coagulated milk separates into pieces, and set aside until the curds have sunk and the whey has separated. Pour off the whey as soon as it forms. Strain the curds after half an hour to remove the rest of the whey.

Mix together 8 eggs, 2 tablespoons of wheat flour, half a quart of cream, 1¼ cups sugar, 3½ ounces blanched and chopped almonds, and 10 bitter almonds.

Pour off any whey that might have formed. Mix the curds and the egg mixture and pour it into a greased mold which will hold 3-4 quarts. Bake at 350°F. for an hour. Cover with foil toward the end if the surface of the cheesecake becomes too dark.

Cheesecakes were often given as presents on special occasions. Guests invited to a wake, for instance, usually brought cheesecakes or pastries to the farm where the wake was held. Ten to fifteen cheesecakes could easily be consumed at one wake.

When a house was being built in the village, all the neighbors came to help to raise the roof in more ways than one! Everybody brought cheesecakes for the party that was given to celebrate the building of the new house.

An old recipe from the western part of Småland specified 1½ cups of sugar and 1¾ cups of flour. The evening milk was brought in from the barn, and was skimmed the next morning. That cream was added later when the curds were mixed with the egg mixture. Less cream is used this way than when whole milk is used and cream is added later.

The amount of almonds included in this recipe is amusingly described: "25 cents worth of almonds, half bitter and half sweet." This recipe may well be at least a hundred years old. If you follow it, there will be quite a difference between the amount of almonds from decade to decade!

This cake should be baked at low temperature for 2 hours, or until high, smooth and perfect. Finally a reminder from Christina Valleria, who in her cook book from the early eighteenth century writes: "N.B. Don't forget to put some cherry leaves in the bottom of the mold, because they add a delicious flavor." She seasoned her cheesecakes with rosewater, cinnamon and sugar.

Fatost—The Poor Man's Cheesecake

The cheesecake's poorest relative comes from Ångermanland. It contains milk, rennet and eggs, but not many eggs, and no cream at all. Thus it is better for you than the more expensive cheesecakes and is also easier to make!

Funnel Eriksson has adapted an old recipe to suit a modern family better. Boil 1⅔ quarts of milk together with 2-3 cinnamon sticks for about 40 minutes. By that time about half of the milk will have evaporated. Let the milk cool until lukewarm. Mix in 2 tablespoons of molasses and 1 egg. Grease an ordinary round cakepan with a little butter and pour in the milk mixture. Then mix in very carefully 2 tablespoons of cheese rennet and let stand in the pan for barely 5 minutes. Bake at 300°F. for about 40 minutes.

This cheese is served lukewarm with preserves and with milk or half-and-half if desired. In the old days this cheese was also sometimes used as sandwich spread. It was common food on mountain-dairy farms, and also belonged among the things guests would bring to weddings and wakes. Cardamom and raisins were also frequently added to this cheese.

Egg Cheese from Bohuslän

Egg cheese is always served at parties in Bohuslän, either as a dessert or smörgåsbord dish. This egg cheese contains milk and eggs that curdle together, but it is still not the least bit similar to cheesecake. The egg cheese is curdled with acid, or to be more exact, it sours and becomes very similar to fresh cheese. The souring agent is obtained from curdled milk, curdled cream, buttermilk or ordinary cream that has been left to sour. Some recipes even use vinegar as a souring agent.

To make egg cheese, a special egg cheese mold is used in Bohuslän and in other parts of southern Sweden. It is a tin mold with small holes in the bottom through which the whey may drain. (See the photograph in the earlier section, "Cheese from Oland.") If no egg cheese mold is available, an ordinary large strainer may be used.

You will need a saucepan which can hold 5 quarts. Beat together 6-7 eggs in the saucepan, add 3 quarts of milk and half a quart of curdled milk or cream, and stir. Put on the highest temperature to begin with while stirring with a wooden ladle, and lower the heat after a while. When the temperature has reached 190°F., the curdling starts. It must not boil! Put the saucepan aside and let stand covered with a lid for about 10 minutes. Pour the curds into the egg cheese mold, which should be placed on a drip pan or something similar to collect the whey.

This egg cheese is served with different kinds of preserved fresh or frozen berries.

Easter Cheese—Also an Egg Cheese

From eastern Finland comes an egg cheese which looks like the one from Bohuslän, but isn't quite the same. It is especially common in the coastal areas east of Helsinki, and it contains fewer eggs, less sugar and more salt.

Boil 5 quarts of milk and add 5 cups of curdled milk mixed with 2 eggs. Leave the saucepan covered on a cutting board until the curds have separated from the whey. Scoop the curds up carefully with a perforated spoon and put them in an ordinary cheese mold lined with a cheesecloth. Add 1 teaspoon of sugar and a little salt. Wrap the cloth around the cheese and place a weight on top. After a couple of hours the cheese is ready to be taken out of the mold.

The cheese may be baked later if so desired. Place it on a greased baking sheet in a hot oven, so that it will quickly turn light brown on the surface.

Chapter 8

Mes Cheese and Mes Butter

Mes is a whey product used in some Scandinavian countries to produce cheese and butter. Whey-butter differs from whey-cheese only in having a slightly higher water content. Whey-cheeses are typical, traditional cheeses of Sweden and Norway.

Vaporization is the process used in the manufacturing of whey products. The whey is heated until most of the water in it has evaporated. Milk sugar (lactose), albumin (a protein), citric acid, milk fat and salts remain. Whey-cheese is a low-fat cheese that is nonetheless high in calories since it consists mainly of milk sugar. In the past, whey-butter was mixed with ordinary sugar, butter and milk, resulting in a product even richer in carbohydrates and fat.

Whey is generally considered a by-product, an undesirable leftover when common rennet cheese is made. But anyone comparing rennet cheese made from sweet milk to whey cheese will soon learn to appreciate the latter. Cow's whey-butter has a mild pleasant taste, and a buttery spreadable consistency if it is boiled for just the right length of time. Many consider whey-butter better than the cheese itself!

Whey—Problem Child of the Dairies

In the past, whey was always carefully saved. A nutrient which could be used for both people and animals was something one could not afford to throw away. Nowadays, however, our standard of living has become so high that whey is being pumped out into lakes or poured into large holes in the ground. In some areas whey is also used for cattle fodder. Whey powder can be mixed with other fodder and pigs can even drink the whey as it is. But thousands of tons of whey are still being disposed of each year.

The mes of the cheese industry is what remains of the whey after its water has evaporated through boiling. It is a product that will keep a long time without preservatives. Whey-cheese containers in Sweden are stamped "fresh" and "will keep five months" but on the store shelves one may find whey cheese up to ten months old.

Whey cheese made at home on the goat farms in Sweden is a product that must be eaten fresh. Here the whey is boiled and made into cheese without the use of chemical additives. This is pure whey-cheese often sold as a gourmet specialty to cheese fanciers. And so it is certainly as possible to make whey-cheese without chemicals in our day as it was in the old days. Although it takes time, it is not difficult.

How Mes Was Made in the Old Days

In the past, whey-cheese was made daily on mountain-dairy farms. As soon as the primary cheese matter had been removed from the pot, the whey was put back on the fire to simmer for many more hours, sometimes until the following day. Cheesemaking differed slightly from village to village—some people boiled the whey only long enough to make it spreadable, while others boiled it until it was so thick that it would solidify after cooling.

Sönning was the name given to the mes when it had been removed from the pot while still soft enough for a skin to form when it cooled. *Messmör* was the *sönning* that had boiled to form the whey-butter. To produce *mesost*, or the whey cheese, the *sönning* had to be boiled still longer. When the solid portion separated from the boiling liquid, it was worked with a spoon or a whisk until cooled, and finally emptied into a mold. When the whey-cheese had thoroughly hardened, the mold was removed.

In Hälsingland, a province in northern Sweden, these harder whey-cheeses were not made every day. From each day's whey softer cheeses were made, which were combined together about every two weeks to make one big batch of the harder cheese. It took three to four hours to heat and boil together the softer, smaller cheese to produce the harder variety. The mixture was stirred constantly to prevent burning. Often many milk maids would help one another when it was time to produce the larger hard cheeses. They would take turns stirring the large (12-gallon) kettles. Large cheeses weighing as much as 20 pounds were made in this way.

In order to be able to keep this cheese to use throughout the winter, it was dried. When it was to be eaten, a piece would be cut off and mixed with milk in order to allow it to spread easily.

How Whey Products Are Made Today

We do as the milk maids did; there isn't a great deal of difference. We choose a saucepan with a thick bottom instead of a copper kettle and put it on the stove instead of hanging it over an open fire as in the old days. It takes less time if the whey is boiled in a flat pan, since the greater the surface, the quicker the evaporation. In the beginning the thickness of the pan is not important; only toward the end of the boiling time is a thick bottom needed to prevent sticking.

The boiling of the whey takes several hours. If one starts with 2 gallons of whey in the morning, the boiling will not be over until the afternoon. But it is all right to leave the whey standing for a day if it has been pasteurized first. The whey should be placed with its pan in cold water to cool it, and left cold during the night.

There are two particularly critical moments in the boiling of the mes: one at the beginning, the other toward the end of the process. When the whey just begins to boil, it can easily bubble over, and should be watched carefully until it simmers down. After a while the foaming will end and the whey can be left to simmer slowly on its own. How the whey boils is less important than how the steam evaporates from it. If the whey is boiled at a high temperature, the evaporation is obviously faster, but this will call for a well-ventilated kitchen to handle the steam. The pot can be left unwatched until the end, when the other critical point arrives—the whey can easily be burned.

The whey is boiled and turns into mes. It takes many hours before all the liquid has evaporated. The curds that rise can be skimmed off and put back into the kettle toward the end of the boiling process.

Just as it starts to bubble, the whey forms a white foam on its surface. This is albumin, a kind of protein, which sinks to the bottom when the whey is boiled. Still more albumin will precipitate after a short while, then in the form of a stiffer foam. This sweet and good-tasting foam is called *vitmese* (white whey). This vitmese is often kept in a bowl, to be added when the whey is nearly done. The risk of burning is less if the albumin is not boiled with the rest of the whey, and the nutritional value of the albumin is also preserved. When the latter is added to whey-butter, the butter has a lighter color than if they had been boiled together.

If time is crucial, it is possible to leave the albumin in the whey throughout the whole boiling process. The result is still a good-tasting whey-butter. The risk of burning can also be considerably diminished by beating it with a whisk just as the albumin is precipitating when it first begins to boil.

Toward the end of the boiling period, it is necessary to increase the stirring of the whey. When it has the consistency of a thin porridge, the albumin is added, unless it was not removed earlier. The mixture must be carefully stirred and the temperature lowered. To check consistency, a spoonful may be poured in a cup and cooled by placing it in cold water while stirring. If whey-butter with a soft, spreadable consistency is desired, the boiling time should be decreased. To produce the harder whey-cheese, which can be sliced with a knife, the whey must be boiled until it reaches a very thick consistency like that of a heavy porridge. It is important to consider that the whey hardens when cooled.

After the kettle is taken from the stove it should be put in a basin of cold water. There the mixture should be worked with a spoon while it cools, until it is completely cold. If this is not done, the milk sugar will form crystals, which will give the whey a granular, rather than smooth texture.

Whey-butter should be put in a glass jar with a lid and kept in the refrigerator. The whey from about 5 quarts of milk should produce about 2 pounds of butter.

If whey-cheese is being made, an oblong loaf-shaped mold is preferable. If you plan to make this cheese often, it would be well worth while to find a collapsible wooden mold, from which it could easily be removed. Otherwise the cheese can be removed by knocking the mold against a cutting board. The Norwegian *primost* recipe calls for the use of a cheesecloth, even for whey cheeses. This is often the easiest way to remove the cheese smoothly from its mold without crumbling.

To smooth the cheese and to even the edges, a wet knife should be used. This done, the cheese is ready to eat. It should be stored covered in the refrigerator. Whey-cheese and whey-butter are fresh products and should not be stored too long; it is possible, however, to freeze them. If the cheese is kept too long, the taste will deteriorate and a mold will form on it, making it unfit for human consumption.

Whey products can be made from the whey of many kinds of milk. Goat whey has a very characteristic, strong taste. A similar taste can be achieved by boiling whey from cow's milk mixed with a small amount of goat milk. Goat whey itself is not really necessary; ordinary sweet goat milk will give the same taste. Pure goat whey-cheese must, on the other hand, be made from goat whey without the addition of sweet milk.

Tips for Burned Saucepans

To wash the saucepan, put it on the stove with a small amount of water and cover. When the water boils, steam forms and the whey deposits soften, making the pans easier to clean once the cheesemaking is over.

Sooner or later, the whey will burn in the pan, so it is good to be prepared. It will happen more easily if the pan has a thin or uneven bottom. Even if only the whey on the bottom is burned, however, the strong smoke taste will spread through the entire pan. Carefully separated unburned whey will still be edible, and some have suggested that its burned taste serves as "a piquant spice"!

Fästmömessmör (fiancé whey-butter) is an old name for burned whey. If the dairy maid is so engrossed in thoughts of her fiancé that she forgets to stir the whey and it burns, *fästmömessmör* is the result.

The saucepan should be allowed to cool first, then filled with warm water, and brushed clean of whatever comes loose. The pan can then be placed on the stove again and heated slowly, keeping a metal dough scraper handy. With luck the entire burned cake will loosen and rise and can be easily scraped clean. If necessary, the procedure should be repeated.

Sötost, Rörost, Pank

The names and variations are many, but basically we are speaking of a sweet cheese dish with a long tradition. Each province claims that the dish is typical for them. The recipes, which vary from one end of the country to the other, are all old enough to be a point of interest in the cultural history of Scandinavia. Today they are prepared only by a few tradition-minded people. It is, however, not at all difficult to prepare *pank* or any of its other variations.

All these dishes are prepared by the addition of rennet to sweet milk, which is then allowed to thicken and congeal. After stirring, the cheese is not removed from the stove but allowed to boil with the whey for a long time. The result is a sweet-tasting mixture to which flour or cream and various spices may be added. It is eaten either lukewarm or cold, as a snack with bread or for dessert on special occasions such as Christmas or Easter.

Sötost

In the northernmost provinces this dish is called *sötost*, sweet cheese. Sweet milk is heated to about 98.6°F. and mixed with rennet. Sweet milk can also be curdled with buttermilk. If this is the case, the milk must first be brought to a boil, as in making fresh cheese, and the sour milk or buttermilk is added later. When the whey appears on the sides of the pan, the mixture must be stirred to prevent early coagulation. A mixture of wheat flour and milk is then added and all is left to boil for some time, until the whey has evaporated and the mixture has turned to a yellow color. At this point, it will be ready to eat with cream, cinnamon and sugar; sometimes it can be spiced with anise.

Rörost

A little further south the same dish is called *rörost*, or stirred cheese. In a recipe for four people, 1 teaspoon of rennet should be added to 1 quart of lukewarm milk. The mixture should be well stirred and boiled. In this recipe the cheese is boiled in the whey until it turns a brown color. Toward the end a thickening agent is added, made up of about 2 tablespoons of cream and 1 teaspoon of wheat flour. In some recipes a cinnamon stick is added to the boiling mixture from the start, and in other variations the thickening is left out.

Try rörost—it is good! The ingredients are milk and rennet. Let the curds boil in the whey, until light brown. Add a little cream mixed with a very little flour, a sprinkling of cinnamon and cardamom and the rörost is ready.

Pank

The recipe for *pank* comes from the provinces of Medelpad and Hälsingland in northern Sweden. It is sometimes incorrectly called *rörost*, but the two differ in color and amount of thickening added. Pank is not supposed to be as brown as rörost and should also contain more thickening and therefore be more solid.

To prepare pank, milk is heated, mixed with rennet and allowed to curdle. A bit of whey is removed as it begins to form and is replaced with milk. A cinnamon stick and whole or ground cardamon are added and the mixture boiled until yellow. Finally, the thickening agent is added and it is ready to serve with cream for extra richness.

A slightly different cheese is obtained by not removing the whey immediately, but letting it boil for about an hour longer with the milk, and then replacing it as above. In some areas rice is added to the pank to make it more filling, or the whey is not removed at all, with thickening and spices added as previously described. In spite of its very sweet taste, sugar is sometimes added, as well as a little salt.

Sötost from Småland

This is the last variation, coming from the southern part of Sweden. Two tablespoons of flour and 2-3 tablespoons of rennet are added to 4-5 quarts of milk. The mixture is then allowed to let stand until it curdles. Then it is cut with a knife, as with ordinary cheesemaking, and left to stand longer. It is heated up quickly in a pan and allowed to boil vigorously while being stirred; then the heat is reduced. The mixture should be stirred until it achieves the consistency of thin porridge; superstition has it that a silver coin in the saucepan will prevent burning. Finally, the cheese is thickened with an egg and a tablespoon of wheat flour, which are whipped in at the end of the stirring. Poured in a bowl and allowed to cool, it is then ready to eat.

Cheese gruel

Cheese gruel, the Swedish *ostvälling*, is pank or sötost in the form of a soup. It contains about the same ingredients as pank with more milk and egg added. The following recipe was submitted by a milk maid from Hälsingland.

Add 3 tablespoons of rennet to 8 quarts of milk. Store-bought milk may be used, but the cheese content in the gruel will be less, and the milk will take longer to curdle. When the milk has curdled, it is whipped and boiled as for pank. After about an hour, half the whey is removed and replaced with about 3 quarts of milk. Add a small amount of ground cinnamon and let boil again. Add sugar to taste, 2 eggs, ⅔ cup of whipping cream, and flour as a thickener. This cheese gruel is served either hot or cold.

A protein-rich sauce made from fresh cheese-yogurt and curdled milk, spiced with herbs is delicious over fresh or boiled vegetables. The Chopska salad with grated cheese on top comes from Bulgaria.

Very rich and delicious is the dessert cheese cake Paskha. In the bowl there is potkäs, a spread made from different kinds of cheese mixed together. In the copper mold is a rich and nutritious cheese cake.

Chapter 9

Goat Cheese and Sheep Cheese

Goat Cheese

The purest, most original cheese that may be bought in Swedish stores is goat cheese, which goat owners themselves manufacture on their farms. Goat cheese is the only Swedish cheese made completely without additives. Some manufacturers don't even use salt, and the cheese contains only milk, rennet and possibly a souring agent in the form of curdled milk.

This rarity is sold in the most exclusive grocery stores in the big cities of Sweden. It is also sold in ordinary grocery stores in northern Sweden, where the stores trade directly with the manufacturers. Finally, goat cheese is sold right on the goat farms.

The goats provide the milk, and from it are made delicious firm goat cheeses weighing up to 4 pounds. These pictures were taken on the goat farm of Björsarv in northern Sweden.

The cheese is made by the goat owners themselves, who have the license to manufacture and sell cheese made from unpasteurized milk. According to law, all milk for cheesemaking must otherwise be pasteurized.

Goat cheese has a peculiar taste which is quite different from the cheese made from cow's milk. It is evident both in the white cheese (the hard rennet cheese) and in the brown mes. One reason for the difference in taste is that goat cheese has no additives,

which most cheese eaters have become accustomed to. Therefore goat cheese has not become an everyday cheese, not even in the villages where it is made. One the other hand, there are goat cheese lovers who would travel, no matter how far, to buy genuine, "no additives added" goat cheese.

Goat cheese has a slightly lower dry-matter content than cow's milk. An important difference is that the fat particles in goat milk don't stick to each other, as they do in cow's milk. Therefore no cream is formed on top when the milk is left standing. Thus all goat cheese is made from whole milk, or "unskimmed" milk. Goat cheeses are made just like cheeses from cow's milk.

On the farms, cheesemaking is still a craft. The milk is heated either on an electric stove or on a wood stove, and molded in old-fashioned wooden molds. But the temperature is now measured by a thermometer, not a finger, and today's goat cheese manufacturers know a great deal more about the chemistry and bacteriology of cheese than the mountain-dairy maids of bygone days. For a novice in the art of cheesemaking, as well as for those who are more accustomed to making their own cheese, it might be interesting to visit a goat farm to watch how the cheese is made.

Sheep Cheese

Sheep have long been raised for the sake of their meat, wool and skin. It was quite common for each farm to have a small flock of sheep to supply the needed wool and meat. In other European countries (more so than in Sweden), the production of sheep milk and the manufacture of sheep cheese have played an important part in agriculture. Many different kinds of sheep

Travelers, especially to Greece and Italy, have learned to appreciate sheep cheese.

cheese are manufactured, almost always according to recipes a thousand years old. The most famous sheep cheese is Roquefort, which was mentioned in the literature of the Roman, Plinius, who lived in the first century A.D.

Feta is a Greek cheese usually made from sheep milk, but sometimes also from goat milk. It is a soured fresh cheese with a strong and salty taste.

Fresh strong sheep cheese is eaten in many of the Balkan countries, but it supposedly originally comes from Bulgaria. Also from Bulgaria comes the famous

Chopska salad, which consists of diced vegetables covered with a mound of grated sheep cheese. The recipe for this is found in the section on "Cheese Dishes."

The good thing about sheep cheese is that its nutrient content is so concentrated—less milk is needed to yield a substantial cheese. Cow's milk and goat milk contain more water. Sheep milk has a higher concentration of dry particles, and thus yields more cheese per quart of milk. There is more of both protein and fat in sheep milk than in either cow's or goat's milk.

It might be exciting for sheep owners to try to make sheep cheese. Sheep may be milked when lambs are weaned from the ewes in the summer. In case a lamb dies, the milk of the ewe may be used for a while. The milk may be frozen while enough is collected for cheesemaking. Milk may be collected from other ewes as well. It is also possible to mix from sheep and cows, if a larger batch is wanted.

Two things have to be kept in mind in making sheep cheese: if the sheep has an udder inflammation, the milk contains a harmful bacteria and is not suitable for human consumption. The milk which the ewe gives shortly after birth is also not suitable for making cheese. The same holds true for cow's milk—the milk from a cow that has just calved is difficult to use.

Sheep cheese is made just like any other kind of cheese. It is suitable for hard cheeses, soft cheeses, fresh cheeses, and mes-butter.

Here is a recipe for a sheep cheese of the blue cheese type, made with liquid green mold culture. Eleven quarts of sheep milk yielded 8 pounds of cheese, according to the recipe submitted by Gertud Westin. As a souring agent ½ cup of curdled milk was used. When the cheese was to be perforated to provide air for the mold cultures, Gertrud noticed that the holes had to be bigger for sheep cheese than for other cheeses. If they were not big enough, they closed, and no air reached the culture. Gertrud also made ordinary hard cheese from sheep milk. It was placed in a salt solution overnight, and was then stored for maturing at 60°F. for 1½ months. However, it was ready to eat after about one month.

Another difference between sheep cheese and goat cheese is that sheep cheese must not be pressed too hard when molded. The cheese will have a softer consistency if it isn't pressed too much or stirred too long after being broken.

Sheep Cheese and Ricotta from Sicily

One of the original sheep cheeses made is the Italian cheese, ricotta. Ricotta is the same cheese which Swedish mountain-dairy maids call white mes; it is the curd which rises when the whey begins to boil after the firm cheese curd has been removed for the hard cheese.

Sheep breeder Nito Grimaldi in the village of Castelluzo, Sicily, milks his 150 ewes by hand, morning and evening from November till June. He milks them outside, and when he takes the milk buckets into the sheep-cote, the shepherd and the sheep return to the pastures in search of food.

Nito heats the milk in a copper kettle over an open fire, since there is no electricity in the sheep-cote. He uses rennet from the rennet bag of a lamb. The hard cheese is formed in wood-fiber baskets, giving the cheese a beautiful design. He puts the kettle with the whey over the fire again, and lets it boil for about an hour. Then he skims off the 4-inch-thick layer of curds that forms on top. This is ricotta.

One may eat ricotta warm, as it comes from the sheep-cote. In this case pieces of bread are put on a plate, and the ricotta is poured on top. Or else it may be eaten cold, as it is when bought in the store.

"Come and eat ricotta," Nito says to his friends. They all accept, because it is considered quite an event to have an opportunity to eat fresh homemade ricotta, direct from the sheep-cote.

Ricotta in a more refined form may be eaten as a dessert cheese, mixed with different flavorings and shaped as a roll similar to spiced butter but with a sweet taste.

Chapter 10

Cheese Dishes

A little grated cheese tastes good with almost anything and may be used in many different ways. Meat, fish and vegetables all taste delicious baked in the oven with a cheese sauce or simply with grated cheese on top. But cheese should not simply be regarded as a flavoring. It is above all an important source of protein, and may very well replace both meat and fish in cooking. Most cookbooks include recipes for cheese dishes, and there are even those which exclusively feature cheese dishes.

We have included some of the more unusual recipes, especially for the use of your own homemade fresh cheese and soured cheese. Fresh cheese made from skim milk is the leanest protein there is.

139

Homemade fresh cheese is furthermore an unusually inexpensive ingredient on which to base a meal. Or the meal could be based on vegetables with fresh cheese added as a protein topping. (Cold fresh-cheese sauce is especially suitable for pouring over raw or boiled vegetables.) Many different kinds of cheese may be mixed into vegetable gratins, salads or used as filling in pies and pancakes.

Cold Fresh-Cheese Sauce

Mix any kind of fresh cheese with a little yogurt and curdled cream or milk into a soft consistency. Add a couple of tablespoons of finely chopped onion, plenty of fresh parsley, dill and chives or other tasty herbs. The sauce should be dotted green all the way through. Season with herb salts. For a more nourishing and filling sauce, try adding a couple of chopped, hard-boiled eggs.

This sauce may be served with raw vegetables or with many kinds of boiled vegetables: potatoes, red beets, carrots, peas, leeks, cabbage and others.

Chopska Salad

This salad originally came from Bulgaria, but many neighboring countries have similar traditional dishes.

Cut green paprika, tomatoes, unpeeled cucumber and fresh onion (ordinary yellow onions may be used) into small uniform pieces. Mix with chopped parsley.

Make a sauce of one part vinegar, three parts of sunflower-seed oil (or any other vegetable oil), one part water and salt to taste. The salt may be left out if the cheese is salty. Mix the vegetables with the sauce and pour plenty of grated cheese on top. Suitable kinds of cheese in addition to the sour sheep cheese of the original recipe are: yogurt-cheese, curdled-milk cheese, white goat cheese and ordinary homemade rennet cheese.

Cheese Pie

Cheese pie, also known as quiche lorraine, may be made in several different ways. The basis is a pie shell filled with a mixture of egg, cheese and milk with spices. The classical quiche lorraine also contains smoked ham. Chopped mushrooms, onion or leeks may also be added. By adding these things the pie becomes more filling.

You may choose your favorite crust recipe or use this crunchy dough made from graham flour: Put 1½ cups of graham flour in a bowl. Use a cheese cutter to slice 3½ ounces of butter into a bowl and work the flour and butter together with your fingers or with a knife or wooden spoon. Add 3 tablespoons of cold water. Roll the pie dough out immediately and line into a greased pie pan. Put it in a cool place for a while. Perforate with a fork so that the dough won't get bubbly while baking, and bake at 425°F. for about 10 minutes.

Mix the filling while the pie crust is baking: 7 ounces of fresh cheese (soured cheese or fresh rennet cheese), 1 or 2 eggs, ½ cup of milk and grated cheese to taste. If a large amount of salty grated hard cheese is added, no salt is necessary. Otherwise, a little herb salt may be added. Oregano, paprika powder, chopped onion or leeks may also be used.

Bake at 325°F. until the filling has stiffened and turned a nice color, which usually takes about 20 minutes.

Cheese Pancakes

The following recipe will provide adequate proportions for two people or a dessert for four. The pancakes should be made small, for larger pancakes break easily when turned.

Crumble 3½ ounces fresh cheese with a fork and mix with ½ cup graham flour and 1¼ cups of milk. Add 1 egg, 3 tablespoons of soya flour, 3 tablespoons of wheat germ, 1 tablespoon of oil and a little salt. Beat the mixture smooth. The batter should preferably stand for a while before it is poured on the griddle, but this is not absolutely necessary. Lightly oil your griddle or fry pan and heat. When it is almost smoking, drop your cakes with a spoon. Remember to make them small. Your cakes are ready to be turned when the tops begin to bubble. You can serve these pancakes as a dessert with berries, honey, syrup and butter. You can also use them as the main course by making a vegetable sauce from onion and tomatoes, cooked together with a little yogurt.

Potkäs

From cheese leftovers a good strong cheese spread may be made. Grate different kinds of strong-tasting hard cheeses. Include crumbled blue cheeses, such as Gorgonzola or green-mold cheese, and a little butter so the mixture forms a smooth spread. Cumin or paprika powder may also be added. A few spoonfuls of brandy or other liquor add to the taste. Pack the mixture into a bowl rinsed with water, and turn upside down onto a platter.

If a pretty color is desired, add the juices from red beets, carrots or green leaves, rather than food coloring!

This dish may be served with fresh vegetables such as cucumbers and radishes or with fruit.

Pashka

This Russian and East European dessert cake is made from *kvark* (a kind of cottage cheese). The smooth fresh cheeses made from curdled milk or långfil are suitable for pashka.

Work together 5¼ ounces of butter and ⅔ cup of sugar. Add 2 egg yolks and stir until smooth. Add 21 ounces of fresh cheese, 3½ ounces of chopped almonds, ½ cup of curdled cream and 1 tablespoon of vanilla. Grated lemon peel, raisins and candied citron peel may also be added for taste.

In Estonia, which now is a part of the Soviet Union, a special pashka mold is used, but an ordinary flower pot may also be used. Lining the pot with a cloth will facilitate removing the pashka. Pack the cheese mixture into the pot and keep cool for at least 24 hours. Then turn it upside down on a platter and decorate the top. In Estonia they sometimes use a paper flower for that purpose. Pashka is eaten at parties for dessert instead of cake.

Appendix

Cheesemaking Suppliers

If you can't find the supplies you need at your druggist or health food store, these companies can supply you with various enzymes, cultures, equipment, and other materials you need. Chr. Hansen's and Dairyland are probably the most comprehensively oriented to individual customers but all can provide some of the things you need. Write for their catalogs, order blanks, and instructional and technical leaflets and bulletins.

Chr. Hansen's Laboratory, Inc.
9015 W. Maple St.
Milwaukee, Wisconsin 53214

In Canada:

Horan-Lally Co. Ltd.
1146 Aerowood Dr.
Mississauga, Ontario L4W 1Y5

In England:

Chr. Hansen's Laboratory Ltd.
476 Basingstoke Rd.
Reading, Berks RG2 0QL

In Australia:

Victorian Rennet Mfg. Col. Pty. Ltd.
16 Queen St.
Munawaging, Victoria 3131

Dairyland Food Laboratories
620 Progress Ave.
Waukesha, Wisconsin 53187

The Diary Laboratories
23rd and Locust Streets
Philadelphia, Pennsylvania 19103

Marschall Dairy Laboratories
P. O. Box 592
Madison, Wisconsin 53701

Countryside General Stores, Ltd.
Hwy 19 East
Waterloo, Wisconsin 53594

Institut Rosell
8480 St. Laurent Blvd.
Montreal, Quebec H2P 2MB

In the United States:

International Yogurt Co.
628 N. Doheny Dr.
Los Angeles, California 90069

For Bulletins on Cheesemaking

Superintendent of Documents
U.S. Government Printing Office
Washington, D.C. 20402

Or:

Government or university departments fostering dairy interests and technology, including "Cooperative Extension" offices of the U.S. Department of Agriculture or state departments of agriculture in many cities—check your telephone directory.

Hints for Perfecting Your Cheese

The Quality of Milk

The quality of milk means everything in cheese making. You cannot make good cheese from poor milk. Be sure of cleanliness in milking, cleanliness in handling the milk, proper cooling of the milk—it should be well cooled but not frozen. See that all utensils used in handling the milk and making the cheese are clean and scalded. Fight flies; they are enemies of good milk. Never make cheese from milk which is already noticeably sour in taste.

Milk which is over-ripened may cause your cheese to become sour in flavor. Cheese made from milk which has not been handled with proper care is very apt to be gassy and have acid, bitter, fruity or other undesirable flavors. If your curd has not been allowed to firm properly, you may get a pasty body, or even a sour cheese. In that case cut the curd into smaller pieces and warm it a bit longer.

Milk for Cheese Making

In making most types of cheese, the milk is generally ripened to contain 0.17—0.20% lactic acid. For ordinary cheese, the proper ripening can usually be accomplished roughly by cooling evening's milk to 50—60°F. in running water, leaving it overnight and mixing with the next morning's milk.

When properly ripened, the milk should not be sour to the taste and should not curdle when boiled. However, a certain degree of ripening is essential in developing a good firm curd.

The riper the milk and the higher the temperature, the less rennet is required, but sufficient rennet must always be used to obtain a firm curd and proper ripening of the cheese. The temperature at which the rennet is added should always be the same for the same type of cheese; it is usually 86°F.

If You Want a Harder Cheese

1. You may cut the curd into smaller pieces.
2. You may hold it a little longer or bring the temperature a little higher.

If You Want a Softer Cheese

1. If your cheese becomes too hard, the reason may be that you have used milk which was over-ripened. Be sure it has not stood too long before you make it into cheese.
2. You may cut the curd into slightly larger pieces.
3. It may be that you can heat to a lower temperature, or not keep it heated as long.
4. Maybe you have used too much weight in pressing.

Chr. Hansen's Laboratory, Inc.

How to Make Neufchâtel Cheese The American Way

Neufchâtel is a smooth, creamy, whole-milk cheese. It is like cream cheese in color, texture, and flavor but has a lower fat content. It is not difficult to make your own Neufchâtel and you can adjust the fat, salt, and moisture content to suit your taste.

Equipment

6-quart double boiler

Food thermometer with a range of at least 60° to 140°F

Measuring cup and spoons

Mixing spoon

Muslin bag, a thin dish towel, or 1 yard muslin or cheesecloth for straining (Boil 5 minutes just before using.)

Colander

Large pan

Clothespins (spring type)

Cheese press or one or two flat, smooth, 12- by 12-inch boards (optional)

15- to 20-pound weight (optional)

Ingredients

These ingredients make about 3½ pounds of cheese.
4 quarts whole milk
Up to 1 pint whipping crean (optional)
½ tablet junket (rennet) dissolved in ⅓ cup water
½ cup commercial cultured buttermilk
2 to 3 teaspoons salt, if desired.

Procedure

1. Pour the milk (and cream, if you want a richer cheese) into the top part of the double boiler. If you use pasteurized milk, heat it to 85°F. If the milk has not been pasteurized, heat it to 145°F., hold it at the temperature for 30 minutes, then cool it quickly to 85°F. by placing the container in iced tapwater.

2. When the milk reaches 85°F., add the dissolved junket and buttermilk. Stir until thoroughly mixed.

3. Let the mixture stand at about 85°F. until the whey has separated from the curd and covers the surface. (You can maintain the temperature by placing the pan in 85°F. water and adding more hot water as needed.) This takes about 5 hours. The curd will break clean from the side of the container when you tip it. The whey should have a sour taste.

4. Cut the curd into strips by running a long thin knife through it as shown in the drawing in the following recipe.

5. Stir well to break up the curd. Heat it to 110°F., stirring gently.

6. Pour hot curd and whey into the muslin bag, with the bag over a container to catch the drained whey. If you do not have a muslin bag, put a towel or cloth in a colander or over the opening of a large pan, using the clothespins to hold the cloth in place. Pour the hot curd and whey into the cloth. Work the curd to the center with a spoon so that the whey drains faster. Collect the whey in a pan.

7. Let the curd finish draining in the muslin bag or cloth for at least 6 hours in the refrigerator. If you want a drier, less acid cheese, let it drain for 12 hours. (The more whey removed, the less acidic will be the final product.) Rather than draining it in the refrigerator, you can also press the cheese to remove the whey.

To press, leave the cheese in the cloth or muslin bag and place it between two boards. Put the weight on top to force out the whey. If you want a drier cheese, use more weight. Maintain the pressure until the curd has a firm, pasty consistency.

8. Keep the whey in the refrigerator until the cream rises and becomes firm enough to skim. The cream will have a butter-like consistency. Work it back into the curd.

9. When the cheese is drained, add salt, if desired, and mix well.

The cheese is now ready to eat. To store Neufchâtel, put it in a covered container or wrap it tightly in foil or plastic wrap, and refrigerate it. It keeps for a week or longer in the refrigerator.

Good Neufchâtel cheese has a mild, clean flavor and a smooth, buttery texture and consistency. When the cheese is too dry, it is usually grainy and lumpy. Too much moisture makes the cheese very soft.

From Leaflet, 2415, Cooperative Extension, University of California and U.S. Department of Agriculture, Berkeley, CA 94720.

John C. Bruhn, Extension Food Technologist, UC Davis.

A Delightful American-Type Hard Cheese

(The recipe can be cut in half, if desired.)

Equipment:

Food thermometer with a range of 32° to 150°F

Large container to hold 5 gallons of milk (enameled metal or other heat-proof utensil; do not use a galvanized container)

Long-handled wooden spoon

Long butcher knife or spatula (long enough so that the blade will reach the bottom of the container without the handle dipping into the curd)

Cheesecloth (boil 5 minutes to kill molds and bacteria that could spoil the cheese)

Cheese press (see figure 2)

Paraffin

Ingredients

These ingredients make 3 to 4 pounds of cheese.

5 gallons sweet, pasteurized, whole milk

2 cups commercial cultured buttermilk

½ tablet cheese rennet or

    1 tablet junket rennet

4 tablespoons salt

½ tablet cheese coloring or

    1 teaspoon yellow food coloring (optional)

153

TOP VIEW

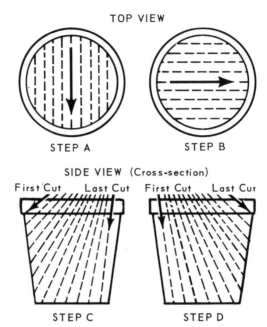

STEP A   STEP B

SIDE VIEW (Cross-section)

First Cut   Last Cut   First Cut   Last Cut

STEP C   STEP D

Cut the curd with a knife. Top view: make perpendicular cuts 1 inch apart, from (step A) back to front and (step B) left to right. Side view, steps C and D: follow cuts of step A as closely as possible, holding knife at angles shown.

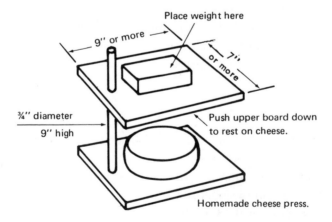

Place weight here

9" or more

7" or more

¾" diameter
9" high

Push upper board down
to rest on cheese.

Homemade cheese press.

From Leaflet 2414, Cooperative Extension, University of California and U.S. Department of Agriculture, Berkeley, CA 94720.

Procedure

1. Pour the 5 gallons of milk into the container. (Both cow's and goat's milk produce good results, but goat's milk gives the cheese a different flavor. You can use low-fat or nonfat milk instead of whole milk, although nonfat milk may slightly change the flavor and reduce the volume of the finished product.)

2. If you prefer yellow cheese, dissolve ½ cheese coloring tablet in ¼ cup cold water and stir into the milk, or stir 1 teaspoon yellow food coloring into the milk.

3. To ripen milk, stir in 2 cups buttermilk.

4. Heat the mixture to 85°F.

5. Dissolve ½ cheese rennet tablet or 1 junket rennet tablet in ¼ cup cold water and stir thoroughly into the milk.

6. Let the mixture stand at about 80°F. until a firm curd forms—about 30 minutes. Test the firmness by inserting your forefinger into the curd and splitting the curd with your thumb. The curd is ready to cut when it breaks evenly over your forefinger and clear whey fills the opening. If the curd is not ready in 30 minutes, it may need more rennet.

7. Use the spatula or knife to cut the curd into cubes of approximately ½ inch. (See drawing.) Let stand 3 minutes without stirring it.

8. To cook the curd, heat slowly to 100° to 105°F. Stir slowly throughout the heating period (about 30 minutes) to prevent the cubes of curd from sticking together and forming lumps.

9. Keep the curd at 100° to 105°F. for an hour, stirring occasionally. Then test the curd for firmness. One indication that it is ready is a squeaky sound when you chew some of the curd. The curd may take another ½ hour or longer to become firm.

10. Pour the whey and curd through cheesecloth placed over a large pan. Drain and discard the whey. When the curd has cooled to 90°F., sprinkle 4 tablespoons salt over the top

of the curd and mix in thoroughly. (You can reduce the salt to 2 tablespoons if you prefer a low-salt product, but the cheese will be bland.) Let the curd stand at room temperature until it forms a mat (1 hour). Cut the matted curd into 1-inch cubes.

11. Place the curd on cheesecloth folded into three or four thicknesses. Wrap the cheesecloth tightly around the curd and pin it in place. Form the curd into a ball.

12. Press the top of the curd down with your hands so that you will be able to get it inside the cheese press.

13. Lay a piece of wet cheesecloth over the top of the curd and place a weight on it. The weight should be about as heavy as a flatiron or brick. (You can make a simple cheese press from two boards and a round stick. See drawing.) Press the curd for ½ hour.

14. Remove the cheese from the press. Cut new cheesecloth to re-cover the cheese completely and as smoothly as possible. First cut two circles that will exactly cover the top and bottom of the cheese. Then cut a strip long enough to wrap around the cheese and wide enough to meet at the center of the top and the bottom over the circular pieces of cloth. Dampen the cheesecloth and apply smoothly to the cheese. Put the cheese back in the press.

15. Place the weight on top and leave it for 8 to 10 hours. Put the cheese on a board and keep in a cool (about 60° to 80°F.), dry place for 4 to 5 days. You can rub the cheese with salt 2 days in succession. Turn the cheese once or twice a day until it forms a rind.

16. When the surface is dry (4 to 5 days), you can cover the cheese with paraffin. Heat the paraffin to 220°F. to keep it from scaling off when the cheese is curing. Dip the cheese halfway into the hot paraffin for about 10 seconds. After the paraffin becomes firm (1 to 2 minutes), dip the other half of the cheese. (Editors note: vegetable oil may also be used as a coating though not as long lasting.)

17. Cheese is better after it has been cured for 4 to 6 weeks. To cure, store it in a dry, clean place at 50° to 55°F.

From Leaflet 2414, Cooperative Extension, University of California and U.S. Department of Agriculture, Berkeley, CA 94720.

Olivia B. Thebus, Home Advisor, Alameda County, California. The author acknowledges the assistance of John C. Bruhn, Extension Food Technologist, UC Davis.